AF207748

SHIPS

Relationships of Life

by
Steve Braswell,
Bill Coffey &
Frank Hamrick

PositiveAction
FOR CHRIST

Copyright © 1987, 1994 by Positive Action For Christ, Inc., P.O. Box 700, 502 W. Pippen St., Whitakers, NC 27891. All rights reserved. No part may be reproduced in any manner without permission in writing from the publisher.

Third Printing 2008
Printed in the United States of America
ISBN: 1-929784-26-0

Designed by Shannon Brown and Jesse Snow

Published by

Foreword

Large boats, called ships, have long been a vital part of the history of mankind. Since our earth is three-fourths water, it was imperative that men learn how to navigate the waterways and thus, the importance of ships. Ships have played an important part in history (ships such as the *Mayflower*, *Monitor* and *Merrimack*, and the *Nina*, *Pinta* and *Santa Maria*). Ships have also had an important role in the accomplishing of God's work (ships such as the ark and the fishing boats of the disciples).

You may not have thought of it before, but God is still using ships today! What are they? They are the relationships of life! How well we get along with God, our parents, our friends and society will determine to a great extent our happiness both here and in eternity!

This study will focus on six different relationships in life, all of which are vital to our well-being. In order, we will study the following:

- KIN*SHIP*—Our Relationship To The Home
- COURT*SHIP*—Our Relationship To The Opposite Sex
- FRIEND*SHIP*—Our Relationship To Our Peers
- SCHOLAR*SHIP*—Our Relationship To Our School
- FELLOW*SHIP*—Our Relationship To The Church
- LORD*SHIP*—Our Relationship With The Lord

As we look at these major relationships, we will come to see how important each is in our lives and that God's Word has clear teaching for us in each of these areas. A teenager who has a right relationship in these six areas will be blessed of the Lord and will possess harmony without and happiness within. This is the kind of teenager the authors of this book trust that the Lord will produce through the use of this study.

Contents

FELLOW*SHIP*: RELATIONSHIP TO THE CHURCH

LORD*SHIP*: RELATIONSHIP WITH THE LORD

SHIPS

Relationships

The Relationships of Life

Great Ships Of The Bible

GREET SHIPS OF THE BIBLE

GREAT SHIPS OF THE BIBLE

• _____ — _____ AND GOD'S _____

NOAH'S ARK — 450 FEET LONG

MAYFLOWER — 90 FEET LONG

ATLANTIC LINER — 860 FEET LONG

THE ARK'S CAPACITY

- Size — _____ feet long, _____ feet broad, _____ feet high
- Displacement — _____ tons
- Gross tonnage — _____ tons
- Could carry the equivalent of _____ railroad cars

GREAT SHIPS OF THE BIBLE

- _____ SHIP — GOD'S _____
- BOAT USED BY _____ — GOD'S _____
- SHIP ON WHICH _____ SAILED — GOD'S _____
  AND _____

THE MOST IMPORTANT SHIPS

Relationship to... _____ — _____ ship
_____ — _____ ship
_____ — _____ ship
_____ — _____ ship
_____ — _____ ship
_____ — _____ ship

The Relationships Of Life

KINSHIP

Keys to success for husbands and wives:

▶ _____ with Spirit
▶ _____ of God

Commands for children:

▶ _____ = _____
▶ _____ = _____

COURTSHIP

The morally impure...
▶Lack _____ (Prov. 6:32)
▶Are _____ (Prov. 7:7)

FRIENDSHIP

"Evil communications
(_____)
corrupt good manners
(_____)"
— 1 Cor. 15:33

SCHOLARSHIP

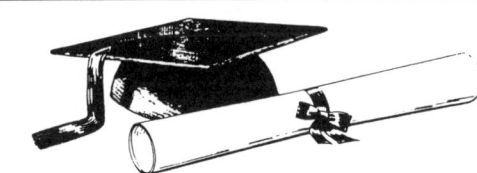

"A wise man will ____
and will _____
_____" — Prov. 1:5

FELLOWSHIP

The local church is God's
earthly representation of
_____.

LORDSHIP

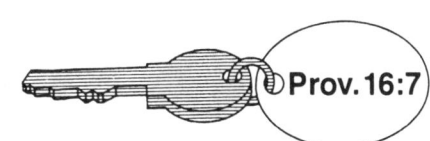

Prov. 16:7

Our relationship with
Jesus Christ is _____
_____
_____.

In the teacher's lesson we introduced the six major relationships of life that we will be studying in ProTeens this year. As we look into God's Word to see what He has to say about each of these relationships, we will learn one major truth—*God is greatly concerned about how well we relate to others.* This is one of the hallmarks of Christianity. God has not called us to isolate ourselves from the world or from each other in order to live the Christian life. Instead, He has called us to learn to relate to other people whether it be at home, at school, at church or in society so that we will be able to minister to their spiritual needs.

One way in which this truth is seen in the New Testament is through the repetition of the phrase "one another." Throughout the pages of the New Testament, we find instructions on how we are to relate to "one another." These instructions are not limited to one particular area of life such as the home or the church, but actually apply to every relationship of life. Notice the following ten commands that deal with our relationships to "one another." Look up the verses beside each command and then fill in the blank(s) provided.

I. _____ ONE ANOTHER (JOHN 13:34-35)

We have placed this command first because it encompasses all the other commands. If we would truly learn to love one another, we would eliminate most of the problems we encounter in our relationships.

II. _____ NOT ONE ANOTHER (ROM. 14:13)

This command does not mean that we should not be discerning in our judgments. It is talking about being quick to pass judgment on others and constantly looking down on other people just because they are not like we are.

III. _____ ONE ANOTHER (ROM. 14:19)

This word means to build up spiritually. Is this true of your relationship to others? Do you build them up spiritually? Is your life of positive beneficial spiritual value to those who know you?

IV. _____ ONE ANOTHER (ROM. 15:14)

This word means to teach, instruct, encourage and warn. This is part of our responsibility to others. It is not enough just for us to know the Word; we must be preparing ourselves to be able to teach it to others also. Whom are you instructing and encouraging spiritually?

V. _____ ONE ANOTHER (GAL. 5:13)

Paul says that we are free from the law, but he also reminds us that we have a duty to serve others. This means that we have to put our plans and our desires aside and think about the needs of others. When was the last time you did something to help someone else even though you really did not feel like doing it?

VI. _____ ONE ANOTHER'S _____ (GAL. 6:2)

What are your burdens? What are the weights on your shoulders that seem almost too heavy for you to bear? Other people have similar burdens, and it is part of our Christian duty to help them carry the weight of those burdens. Do you know someone who has a rough home life or who has trouble with their school work? Be a Christian, and help them bear that burden.

VII. _____ ONE ANOTHER (EPH. 4:32)

Has someone wronged you? What have you done to them in return? God says that we are to forgive the offenses of others. And what right does He have to tell us to do that? For one thing, He Himself is the best example of forgiveness because He has already forgiven us for *all* of our sins.

VIII. _____ TO ONE ANOTHER (EPH. 5:21)

One way we can obey this command is by showing respect to the various authorities under whom God has placed us. That includes your parents, your teachers, your youth pastor and even the city police.

IX. _____ ONE ANOTHER (1 THESS. 4:18)

Life is full of sorrows. God says that it is part of our responsibility to ease the sorrows of our fellow believers by comforting them. Do you know someone who is sorrowing because his family is poor or because he is not shown love at home? Do something to help comfort him in his sorrow.

X. _____ YOUR _____ ONE TO ANOTHER (JAMES 5:16)

This command means that we need to be open and honest with others. Be willing to admit when you are wrong. Anyone can lie, but it takes a real man to be willing to say, "I was wrong, and I'm sorry I did it."

SHIPS

Kinship

Relationship to the Home

The Importance Of The Home

THREE GREATEST INFLUENCES IN LIFE

_____ life

_____ life

_____ life

The most important influence in a teen's life is _____ _____. The most important factor in that influence is not the _____ or _____ condition of the parents, but the teen's _____- _____ toward his home situation.

This is seen in the following:
- God's _____ to children
- The _____ of a wrong attitude

This is the first of six lessons that deal with a subject that hits us right where we live—the home. Perhaps no other factor in a Christian's life influences his future more than the home. The home is important for the following three reasons.

I. THE HOME IS ONE OF GOD'S TWO BASIC INSTITUTIONS

Read Matthew 16:18 and name the other basic institution of God: _____.
Which of these two institutions was formed first? _____ Thus, the home is God's most basic structure. Everything in society is built on the home. As the home goes, so goes the church, so goes the government and so goes the nation. When the home structure collapses, all other institutions will fail.

II. THE HOME AFFECTS THE LIVES OF THE PARENTS

Look up the following verses and record the effects your wise or foolish actions have on your parents.

• The Wise Child

Proverbs 10:1 _____

Proverbs 15:20 _____

Proverbs 23:24-25 _____

• The Foolish Child

Proverbs 10:1 _____

Proverbs 15:20 _____

Proverbs 17:21 _____

Proverbs 17:25 _____

Thus, the happiness and success of the parents is often measured by the children they produce.

III. THE HOME AFFECTS THE LIVES OF THE CHILDREN

What does Proverbs 11:29 tell us about the person who troubles his own household?

_____

To "inherit the wind" is like saying, "You shall inherit nothing but hot air." God has promised that He will never bless a teen who is rebellious inwardly or outwardly toward his parents.

What does Hebrews 12:14 tell us to do that can apply here?_____

_____

_____

_____

If you do not cause peace, but instead cause heartache, worry and concern, and if you are not at peace in your own heart with your parents, what will spring up in your heart? (Hebrews 12:15)_____

This bitterness begins in the home toward your parents or brothers and sisters. Since it begins as a root in your life, it soon grows like a cancer until it gradually affects your relationship with your teachers, your preacher, your friends and all of society; and you become a hardened, bitter, rebellious person. Note Hebrews 12:15 again: The "_____ of _____ " will not only trouble you, but many will be "_____" by it. That is, it will affect everyone around you!

Victory In The Home

HOW SATAN GAINS ENTRANCE INTO OUR LIVES

Devotional life
Social life
Home life

Devotional life
Social life
Home life

Devotional life
Social life
Home life

Through our
_____
life

Through our
_____
life

Through our
_____
life

FOUR STEPS TO VICTORY
1 PETER 5:8-9

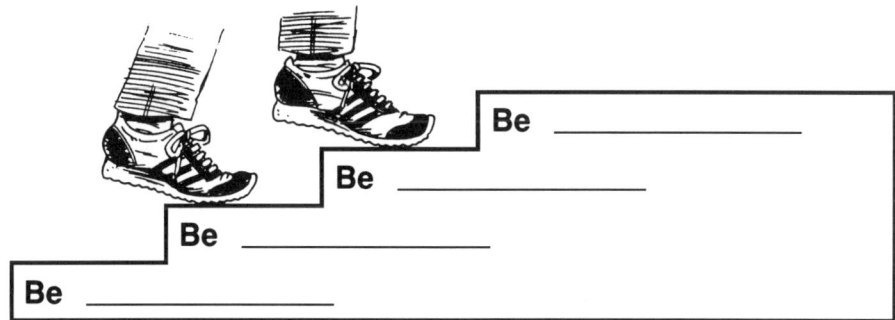

Be _____

Be _____

Be _____

Be _____

I. MISCONDUCT IN THE HOME BRINGS GRAVE CONSEQUENCES

Read the following verses and list beside each the consequences God has promised to bring on those who have improper actions and attitudes in the home.

Proverbs 11:29 _____

Proverbs 15:10 _____

Proverbs 20:20 _____

Proverbs 30:17 _____

Thus, parents who allow disrespect and disobedience to go unchecked are promoting the destruction of their own children.

II. OBEDIENCE BRINGS GREAT REWARD

A. IT PLEASES GOD

Complete from Colossians 3:20: "Children,_____ your parents in_____ _____: for this is _____ unto the Lord." Teenager, do you want to please God? Then obey. To obey your parents, whom God has placed over you, is to obey the Lord.

B. IT PREPARES FOR LIFE

This point will be covered more thoroughly in next week's lesson. The Bible teaches that submission and obedience are foundational to successful living. The teenager who does not learn how to submit to authority will have problems throughout the rest of his life.

C. IT PROTECTS FROM SATAN

What does God say is as the sin of witchcraft? (1 Samuel 15:23) _____ The authority structure in the home provides protection for the children in the home. When you choose to step outside the authority of your parents, you are placing yourself in a position of direct satanic attack. This is what is meant by the phrase we noted in 1 Samuel 15:23. Just as getting involved with the occult opens you up to satanic activity, so does rebellion against authority.

Don't be foolish. Stay under the protection of your parents' authority. Submit to them and obey them, and you will be protected from Satan's attacks.

Do you honestly love, honor and respect your parents? If not, get it settled before it robs you of any more of God's blessings.

Your Place In The Home

GOD'S CHAIN

VERTICAL

1

2

3

4

OF COMMAND

_____

_____

_____

_____

GOD'S WILL FOR YOUR LIFE

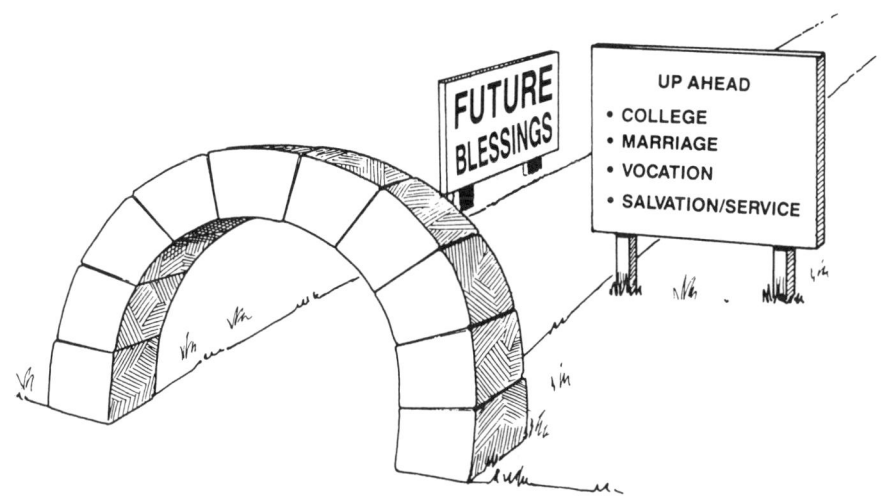

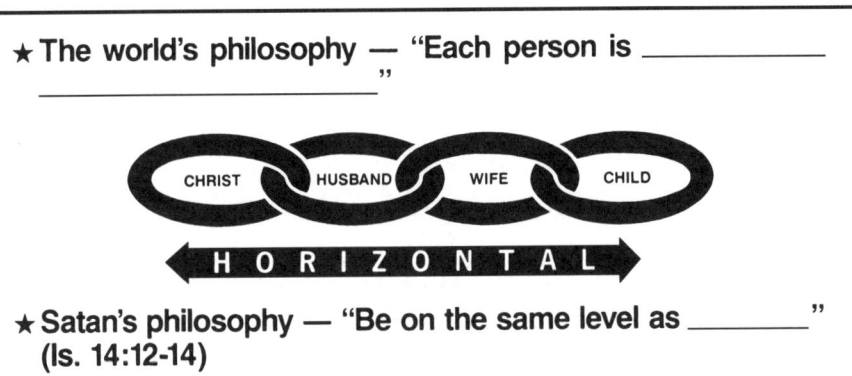

★ The world's philosophy — "Each person is _____ _____"

★ Satan's philosophy — "Be on the same level as _____" (Is. 14:12-14)

Results:
• College — _____
• Marriage — _____
• Vocation — _____
• Salvation — _____ /Service — _____

We have studied the importance of our home life and how it affects our personal welfare. We learned about the "root of bitterness" that begins in the home and "springs up" to ruin our whole lives. In this lesson we will learn how to overcome part of our bitterness by realizing our position in the home. If you learn these facts and practice them in your home, you will be wise and have a happy home life.

I. GOD'S ORDER IN THE HOME

Bitterness in the home is most often caused by our failure to understand and accept God's place for us in the home. God has an order for the chain of command in the home. Read 1 Corinthians 11:3, Ephesians 5:22-25 and 6:1-2. What is God's chain of command in the home?

1._____

2._____

3._____

4._____

II. OUR VARIED RESPONSIBILITIES IN THE HOME

A. THE HUSBAND

According to Ephesians 5:25, what is the husband's first responsibility in the home?

_____

How is he to do this? _____

_____

What did Christ do for the church that provides an example for how the husband is to act toward his wife?

_____

_____

What are some practical ways in which a husband

can show his love for his wife?

_____

_____

_____

B. THE WIFE

According to Ephesians 5:22 and 24, what is the wife's first responsibility to her husband?

_____

How is she to do this according to verse 24?

_____

_____

_____

_____

C. THE CHILD

According to Ephesians 6:1-2, what are the first two responsibilities of the child in the home?

_____

_____

Read the following verses and state what a wise teen will do.

Proverbs 4:1 _____

_____

Proverbs 15:5 _____

_____

According to Proverbs 6:22, what three things will your parents' instructions do for you?

_____

_____

_____

According to Proverbs 6:23, what three things does God call the instructions and commands of parents?

_____

_____

III. SELF-EXAMINATION

Be honest. How do you react toward your father's instructions and advice?

_____

_____

_____

_____

How do you react toward his correction and punishment? _____

_____

_____

_____

How do you react toward your mother's instruction and advice? _____

_____

_____

_____

Is there a problem with your attitude toward your parents? If so, ask God to give you a lowly and meek spirit and to help you accept your place in the home.

Understanding Your Parents

TEACHER'S LESSON

FIVE FACTS ABOUT DISCIPLINE IN THE HOME

- Discipline is _____ and _____ (Prov. 3:12; Heb. 12:7)
- Discipline is _____ (Prov. 23:13)

TWO ILLUSTRATIONS OF DISOBEDIENCE TO THIS COMMAND

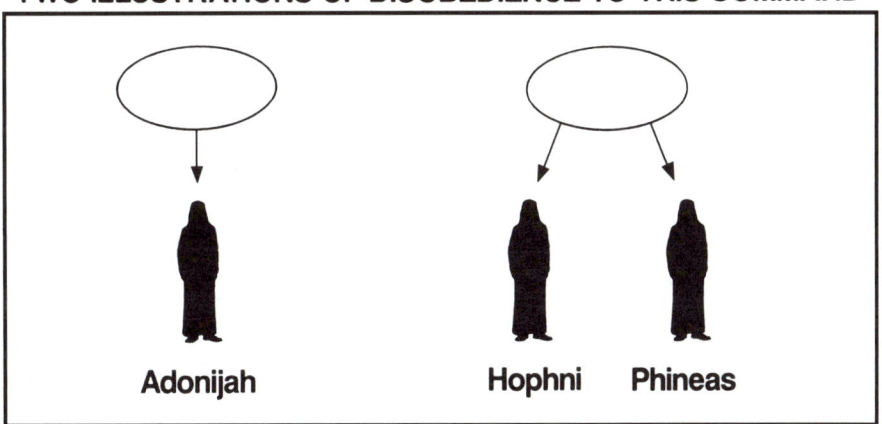

Adonijah   Hophni   Phineas

■ Discipline is due to _____ (Prov. 3:12; 13:24; Heb. 12:6)

> Parental _____, rules and regulations are not meant to _____, but are intended to _____.

■ Discipline produces _____

DISCIPLINE DRIVES OUT...	DISCIPLINE INSTILLS...
• _____ (Prov. 20:30) • _____ (Prov. 22:15) • _____ (Prov. 23:13-14)	• _____ (Prov. 22:6): "Doing what you _____ _____, _____ _____ whether you feel like it or not" • _____ (Prov. 29:15)

■ The most important factor in discipline is _____ (Prov. 3:11; Heb. 12:5)

I. MISTREATING YOUR PARENTS

Have you ever accused your parents of not understanding you? Most teens raise this battle cry at some point in their lives. But have you ever considered that understanding is a two-way street? *Do you understand your parents?* Many teens mistreat their parents because they do not understand them. Read the following verses and state the things you can do to harm or mistreat your parents.

•How Teens Often Mistreat Their Mothers

Proverbs 15:20 _____

Proverbs 19:26 _____

Proverbs 20:20 _____

Proverbs 28:24 _____

•How Teens Often Mistreat Their Fathers

Proverbs 15:20 _____

Proverbs 19:26 _____

Proverbs 20:20 _____

Proverbs 28:24 _____

II. UNDERSTANDING YOUR PARENTS

In order to be a blessing to your parents rather than mistreat them, you must understand three things about them.

A. THEIR LOVE AND UNDERSTANDING

1. Seen In Their Emotions

According to Proverbs 17:6, 21 and 25, is there any connection between the emotions of your parents and your behavior?_____ What does this indicate?

_____

_____

2. Seen In Their Discipline

According to Proverbs 3:12, what strange thing does love cause a parent to do?

_____

According to Proverbs 13:24, what does a father who does not love his child do?

_____

Why else will a parent often fail to discipline a child? (Proverbs 19:18)

_____

What does God tell this soft-hearted parent to do?

_____

Believe it or not, you should thank God for your parents if they are strong disciplinarians. They are simply being obedient to God, and they are doing so out of love and understanding for you.

What if you saw a baby crawling toward a fire, what would you do? What if the baby got mad and cried because you would not let him get near the fire? Would you still say no? What a cruel person you are! You are not letting the baby "do his own thing." You just don't understand him! You don't want him to have any fun! Don't you realize that babies like fire? Of course you know all this, but you know something that the baby doesn't know. You know what fire will do to him. Your love and understanding of the situation causes you to tell the baby no and, if necessary, to discipline him further.

Apply this to your parents. They understand you more than you think they do. Why? Because they have been teenagers—but remember, you have never been a parent! So they understand more about how you feel and why you do the things you do than you can understand about why they do the things they do.

B. THEIR SACRIFICES FOR YOU

You will not realize how much your parents have given up for you until you have children

32

of your own. Talk with your parents and list five things they have sacrificed for you.

_____

_____

_____

_____

Read Hebrews 12:2. What does this verse say about Christ's sacrifice and how He over-looked His pain?

_____

_____

Christ's love for us and His desire to see us saved was so great that His sacrifice, horrible and painful as it was, was faced bravely and joyfully. Your parents' sacrifices for you are but a shadow of this great love Christ has for you.

C. THEIR HUMAN FRAILTIES

Have your parents ever mistakenly punished you? _____ If they are human, they have! Have you held this against them? _____ Why let bitterness develop over human faults and frailties? We are all sinners. If this has been a problem in your life, confess your wrong attitude both to the Lord and to your parents.

III. YOUR RESPONSIBILITY

According to Ephesians 6:1-2, what is your twofold responsibility toward your parents?

_____

Do you honestly, cheerfully and faithfully fulfill your God-given responsibility to them?____

Duties Of The Parents (Part 1)

■ The husband and wife are _____

Marriage involves both…
• _____ your parents
• _____ to your mate

■ **The husband is to...**
- _____ his wife (Eph. 5:22-24)
- _____ his wife (Eph. 5:25)

■ **The wife is to be _____-_____ to her husband's leadership in her...**
- _____ (1 Pet. 3:1-2)
- _____ (1 Pet. 3:3-4)

This lesson deals with the shared duties of the mother and father toward their children.

I. TO TEACH

According to Deuteronomy 6:6-7, what are parents to teach their children? _____

_____

How are parents to teach? _____

When are parents to teach? _____

_____

_____

_____

II. TO TRAIN

According to Proverbs 22:6, in what way is a parent to train his child? _____

_____

As he grows older, what does God say a well-trained child will do? _____

_____

There are two possible meanings for the phrase "the way he should go": (1) it means that parents are to train their children in God's way that He has laid out for them in His Word, or (2) it means that parents are to train their children according to the bent of their inclinations (that is, their gifts, desires and abilities).

If we apply both meanings, we cannot miss being right in our application. Thus, a parent has the responsibility to train his children in the Word of God *and* to encourage the child to develop the abilities with which the Lord has blessed him. (This is why Bible study and lessons in piano, voice, art and speech along with the development of any other special abilities you may have are so important. All of this is part of your parents' responsibility to train you in the right way.)

III. TO PROVIDE FOR

According to 2 Corinthians 12:14, who is to provide for whom?_____

_____

List at least five things that your parents have provided for you. _____

_____

_____

_____

Are you grateful for all that your parents have provided for you? _____

How are you showing them your gratitude?_____

_____

_____

_____

IV. TO DISCIPLINE AND INSTRUCT

We learned in last week's teacher's lesson that discipline is natural and correct and is commanded by God. What word in Ephesians 6:4 means "discipline"?_____
What word in this verse means "instruction"? _____
Parents are to bring their children up with a balance of discipline and loving instruction.

V. TO CONTROL

Paul gave the qualifications for pastors and deacons in 1 Timothy 3:1-13. Thus, before a man is to become a pastor or a deacon, he should make sure that these things are true in his life. However, these are not just standards for church leaders; they should actually be true of every Christian parent.

According to 1 Timothy 3:4 and 12, what is a father to rule well?_____

_____
It is God's plan that your parents exercise control over you and that you submit to that control.

VI. TO LOVE

According to Titus 2:4, what are young mothers to be taught in regard to their children?

_____

This, of course, applies to both parents. It is part of your parents' responsibility before God to show their love for you.

If you have parents who are seeking to be obedient to their God-given duties as a parent, you should be thankful. Since God has commanded them to be responsible to Him in these areas, make sure that you cooperate with them. Do not make it hard for them to do for you what God expects of them.

Duties Of The Parents (Part 2)

■ The wife is a _____ to her husband (Prov. 12:4)

- Prudent in _____ (Prov. 14:1)
- _____ (Prov. 31:11-12)
- _____ and _____ (Prov. 31:20,26)
- Delights in his _____ and _____ (Prov. 31:23)
- _____ (Prov. 31:27-28)
- _____ the Lord (Prov. 31:30)
- _____ (Eph. 5:22-23)
- Immovable in _____ (Tit. 2:4)
- _____ (Tit. 2:5)
- Covers _____ (1 Pet. 4:8)

■ **The husband is a** _____ **to his wife (Eph. 5:23-29)**
This means that he meets her needs...
- _____
- _____

WHAT TO REMEMBER WHEN CHOOSING A WIFE

_____ (_____) **is deceitful, and**
_____ **is vain: but a woman that** _____
_____, **she shall be praised.**
—Proverbs 31:30

I. YOUR PARENTS' SEPARATE RESPONSIBILITIES

God lists some duties and responsibilities for the husband that do not apply to the wife, and some duties for the wife that do not apply to the husband. Thus, although the husband and wife are "one flesh," they have separate responsibilities.

A. THE HUSBAND'S RESPONSIBILITIES

Read each verse below and state what each teaches about the husband's responsibility.

Proverbs 3:12 _____

Proverbs 31:11 _____

_____

Proverbs 31:28 _____

Ephesians 5:25 _____

B. THE WIFE'S RESPONSIBILITIES

According to Proverbs 14:1, what is a wise wife's duty?

_____

This implies that her chief responsibilities involve the interior of the home including its cleanliness, order and comfort.

According to Ephesians 5:22 and 24, what is the wife's chief responsibility toward her husband?

_____

According to Proverbs 4:3, what does a mother bring to the home that a father cannot seem to provide? _____

According to Proverbs 31:14 and 21, for what two things is a wife especially responsible?

_____

41

II. YOUR PARENTS' SHARED RESPONSIBILITIES

There are some areas of responsibility in which Mom and Dad share equally. According to Proverbs 4:1 and 6:20, what responsibility is given to both parents? _____

_____

According to Proverbs 31:28, what is a husband to do for his wife? _____

According to Proverbs 31:12, what does the wife, in turn, do for her husband? _____

_____
Thus, the husband and wife share the responsibility of living their lives, not for their children, but for each other.

III. MOM AND DAD'S GREATEST PROBLEMS

A. MOM'S GREATEST PROBLEM

According to Ephesians 5:31, a man is to _____ his parents and _____
to his _____ , and they shall be _____.
According to this verse, are parents and children bound together for life as one flesh? ____

Here is Mom's greatest problem: she doesn't want Junior to leave. Yet her responsibility from the day her children are born is to prepare them to leave. She is her husband's flesh and belongs to him, not to her children. If your mom is the clinging type, try to understand. All moms are the same. Your mom is working at it, but it doesn't come easily.

B. DAD'S GREATEST PROBLEM

Dad's greatest problem is often in the area of discipline. Though he is commanded to discipline, he will often be guilty of either (1) under-disciplining or (2) over-disciplining. According to Ephesians 6:4, what is Dad's problem relative to discipline? _____

_____
Though your dad may not always discipline as he should, remember that the discipline he does administer is meant to be for your benefit!

SHIPS

Courtship

Relationship to the Opposite Sex

Developing A Proper Attitude Toward Sex

TEACHER'S LESSON

SEX IS NOT SINFUL BECAUSE GOD CREATED...

- _____ (Gen. 1:28)
- _____ (Ps. 139:14)

GOD'S TWO PURPOSES FOR SEX

- _____ (Gen. 1:28)
- _____ (Song 4:1-5:1)

Sex was given to be an _____ expression of the God-given _____ between a man and a woman.

GOD'S PLAN FOR SEX

(1 Cor. 7:1-5; Eph. 5:22-33)

THREE TRUTHS ABOUT MARRIAGE

- It is _____
- It is _____
- It is _____

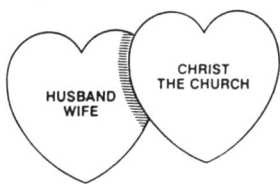

According to Genesis 2:18, what was not good about the man God had created? _____

_____

What did God do according to Genesis 2:21-22? _____

_____

According to Genesis 2:25, who was naked and not ashamed? _____

_____

According to Genesis 1:27-28, what did God instruct the man and woman to do so that the earth might be replenished (filled)?

_____

_____

According to Hebrews 13:4, what is "honorable in all"? _____

According to Hebrews 13:4, what does God say is "undefiled"? _____
(This refers to sex in marriage.)

According to Hebrews 13:4, what will God do to those who practice sex outside of marriage (whoremongers and adulterers)?

_____

According to the verses we have studied in this lesson, who created sex? _____

In what relationship does God permit sex? _____

List three truths you learned about marriage in the teacher's lesson.

1. Marriage is _____.

2. Marriage is _____.

3. Marriage is _____.

Developing A Proper Attitude Toward Dating

THREE STAGES IN THE DEVELOPMENT OF RELATIONSHIPS

	CHRIST AND THE CHURCH	MALE AND FEMALE
SPIRITUAL RELATIONSHIP		
EMOTIONAL RELATIONSHIP		
PHYSICAL RELATIONSHIP		

THREE ESSENTIALS TO SPIRITUAL DATING

1- The right _____ → • _____ (2 Cor. 6:14)
                                • _____ (1 Cor. 5:9-11)

2-The right _____ → Your _____ (Eph. 6:1-3)

                                • _____
                                  _____ (1 Cor. 10:31)

3-The right _____ → • _____
                                  _____ (1 Cor. 14:26)

                                • _____
                                  _____ (Lk. 2:52)

Proper biblical dating must meet four criteria as noted below.

1. GOD MUST BE EXALTED

According to 1 Corinthians 10:31, what is to be your motive in all that you do?

_____

_____

2. CHRISTIAN LOVE MUST BE EXERCISED

Read 1 Corinthians 13:4-8. These verses list sixteen characteristics of love. According to these verses, love...

- Is patient
- Shows kindness
- Is not possessive
- Does not seek attention
- Is not proud
- Does not act shamefully
- Is not selfish
- Is not easily angered
- Is forgiving
- Hates sin
- Loves righteousness
- Protects
- Is not suspicious
- Hopes the best for others
- Endures suffering
- Never ceases

Using some of these characteristics, write a summary of how true Christian love would affect one's dating life.

_____

_____

_____

_____

_____

3. OTHERS MUST BE EDIFIED

To *edify* means "to build up." It is used figuratively for the promotion of spiritual growth. In our relationships with others we should seek to live in such a way as to promote spiritual growth in their lives. This includes dating!

According to Romans 15:2, what is the good for which we should seek to please our neighbor?

_____

According to Romans 14:19, what are the things we are to follow after in our relationships with others?

_____

_____

4. THE HOLY SPIRIT MUST ENERGIZE

What command is given to the Christian in Ephesians 5:18?

_____

The word *filled* contains the idea of "control." The indwelling Spirit of God is the One who should continually control and dominate the life of the believer. As you allow the Spirit to control your life, you will begin to manifest the fruit of the Spirit. When you do not allow the Spirit to control you, the works of the flesh (Galatians 5:19-21) will be manifest.

List the fruit of the Spirit found in Galatians 5:22-23.

(1) _____   (6) _____

(2) _____   (7) _____

(3) _____   (8) _____

(4) _____   (9) _____

(5) _____

Therefore, to have the right relationship with others, we must allow the Holy Spirit to control our lives.

Developing A Proper Attitude Toward My Body

TEACHER'S LESSON

BEFORE YOU DATE...

Understand your _____

- You have a _____

Aroused by
_____

Aroused by
_____

A Christian young lady should never dress in a way that draws attention to _____ that invite _____ in a young man.

- This sex drive was given for _____

BEFORE YOU DATE...

Understand the danger of _____

(1 Cor. 6:9-18; 7:1-5)   (1 Th. 4:3-7)

FOUR TRUTHS ABOUT THE BODY AND SEXUAL AROUSAL

- ✓ The body is made to _____.
- ✓ The amount of _____ will determine the degree of _____.
- ✓ The degree of _____ will determine the amount of _____.
- ✓ The result of defrauding is _____, _____ and _____ in the relationship.

 **BOY A**   **GIRL A**

 **GIRL B**   **BOY B**

Treat every _____ as though he or she were another person's _____.

According to Romans 6:6, what has been crucified with Christ? _____

_____

The *old man* is all that a person was before he was saved.

What does Romans 6:6 say has been destroyed? _____

The *body of sin* means the human body controlled by sin. The word *destroyed* means "to be made ineffective." This does not mean that the body in and of itself is sinful, but that before salvation, it is controlled by sin. At salvation the controlling power of sin is broken and rendered inoperative. This does not mean that you no longer have the capacity to sin. You still have the sinful nature; but since you have been set free from its power, you no longer have to obey it.

According to Romans 6:11, what are you to reckon yourself to be in regard to sin?

_____

According to Romans 6:11, what are you to reckon yourself to be in regard to God?_____
(The word *reckon* means "to count it to be so.")

What is a Christian commanded to do in regard to sin according to Romans 6:12-13?

_____

_____

According to Romans 6:13, what are you commanded to do in regard to God? _____

_____

_____

According to 1 Corinthians 6:13, for whom were our bodies created? _____

According to 1 Corinthians 6:13, for what was your body *not* created? _____

_____

What are you commanded to do in 1 Corinthians 6:18? _____

_____

According to 1 Corinthians 6:19-20, who lives in the Christian's body? _____

_____

What are we to do with our bodies according to verse 20? _____

_____

Setting Proper Dating Standards

YOU ARE OLD ENOUGH TO DATE WHEN YOU KNOW...

• The _____ and _____ of dating

BENEFITS	DANGERS

YOU ARE OLD ENOUGH TO DATE WHEN YOU HAVE...

• Established _____ from _____

3 REASONS FOR ESTABLISHING STANDARDS

• You will give an _____ of yourself to God (Rom. 14:12)
• You will _____ what you _____ (Gal. 6:7-8)
• God's way is always _____ (Ps. 145:17)

5 AREAS OF DATING THAT DEMAND STANDARDS

• _____ you will date
• _____ you will date
• _____ you will date
• _____ you will date
• How you will _____ on a date

YOU ARE OLD ENOUGH TO DATE WHEN YOU...

• Have your _____ approve your _____
• Have _____ in your heart not to _____ your standards even if it means _____.

To some, this study may seem boring and uninteresting; to others, it will be of utmost importance. Some of you have been dating for quite some time; others have just started; still others certainly wish they could, and some couldn't care less. However, at some time in the very near future, what is studied here will be vital in the life of every teenager.

The teacher's lesson discussed four factors that must be considered before you are old enough to date. Your student's lesson looks at two of these.

I. I MUST HAVE PROPER DATING STANDARDS

Now you may ask, "What things do I need to have standards about?" Below are listed several questionable areas that will become evident as you begin to date. Beside each activity, list at least two verses that give you a standard and state in your own words what that standard is. This is a difficult assignment, we realize, but serious and prayerful consideration and study will increase your spiritual maturity and dedication to the Lord. Here are some verses for you to use in forming your biblical dating standards.

- Psalm 101:3
- Proverbs 13:20; 14:23
- Matthew 6:33
- Romans 12:1-2; 13:14; 14:13, 21-23
- 1 Corinthians 5:9-11; 6:18-20; 7:36; 10:31; 15:33
- 2 Corinthians 6:14-17
- Ephesians 5:10-11; 6:1-3
- Colossians 1:28-29; 3:17
- 1 Thessalonians 4:3-7; 5:22-23
- 1 Timothy 2:9
- 2 Timothy 2:22
- Hebrews 10:25; 13:17

Here are some areas to consider. On the lines provided below each category, write your standard in your own words and list two Scripture references that support that standard.

A. WHOM I WILL DATE

_____

_____

_____

_____

B. WHY I WILL DATE

_____

_____

_____

_____

C. WHEN I WILL DATE

_____

_____

_____

_____

D. WHERE I WILL GO ON MY DATES

_____

_____

_____

_____

WHOM? WHY? WHEN?

E. HOW I WILL CONDUCT MYSELF ON MY DATES

_____

_____

_____

_____

II. I MUST MAKE THESE STANDARDS MINE

You have established biblical standards for dating, but that is not enough. It is one thing to have standards, but it is quite another thing for those standards to become yours. Thus, a person is old enough to date when he has purposed in his heart that these standards are his; and they will not be lowered, even if it means losing dates.

How do we purpose in our hearts to do or not to do certain things? You may say, "I've tried that before, and I always break the promise I make to myself." Note Daniel 1:8. What did Daniel do before he ever encountered temptation among the Babylonians?

_____

Notice also what David said in Psalm 108:1: "_____

_____

_____ "

Both men settled their standards beforehand. They had already determined what they would do in each situation. So when that situation arose, they acted in accordance with what they had already settled in their hearts.

You now have your standards, but have you purposed with true dedication that you will abide by these standards? _____ If you are really serious, carefully and prayerfully make a vow to the Lord that you will not break His standards for your life. Warning! Before you do this, read Ecclesiastes 5:4-7 and state in your own words what these verses mean.

_____

_____

_____

_____

SHIPS

Friendship

Relationship to Our Peers

I Need A Friend

TEACHER'S LESSON

- Ex. 24:13; 32:17; 33:11

- Ruth 1:14-18

- 1 Sam. 18:1-4

- 2 Ki. 2:1-8

- Dan. 1; 2:48-49

- Mt. 17:1; 26:37

- 2 Tim. 4:9

THE DEFINITION OF A FRIEND

A friend is a _____
with whom I share _____,
who _____ me in spite of what I do and whose
influence helps me achieve _____
for my life.

FOUR LEVELS OF FRIENDSHIP

Level Of Friendship	Type Of Communication

THE BASIS FOR ALL FRIENDSHIPS

APPROVED

- All Friendships should be _____ by Jesus Christ.
- Right relationship with_____ = Right relationships with_____

Over the next few weeks we will be studying the topic of friendship. During these weeks you will be assigned simple projects for you to complete that will have something to do with friendship. As you complete each project, turn it in to your youth director. For each completed "Friendship Project" you will receive 50 points. These points count for Local Scoring only and not for ISC.

FRIENDSHIP PROJECT #1

Copy the following chart five times. Write the name of one of your friends in the top section of each chart. After each name give the following information: (1) the interests that you have in common with that friend, (2) the one thing you like best about that friend and (3) what you can do to be a better friend to that person. After you complete the charts, take another look at them. What do these charts tell you about yourself? What do they tell you about the way you choose your friends?

FRIEND'S NAME	
OUR COMMON INTERESTS	
WHAT I LIKE BEST ABOUT THIS FRIEND	
WHAT I CAN DO TO BE A BETTER FRIEND TO THIS FRIEND	

The Friendship Of Jonathan And David

CHARACTER OF JONATHAN

1. Was _____

2. Took the _____

3. Had _____ in his God

4. Had the _____ of others

DO YOUR FRIENDS HAVE THESE QUALITIES?

CHARACTER OF DAVID

1. Willing to perform _____ tasks
2. Empowered by the _____ of God
3. Had a good _____

  • Skillful _____
  • _____, _____ man
  • Man of _____
  • _____ in _____
  • _____ man
  • _____ man
4. Had _____
   in his _____

In the teacher's lesson we looked at the friendship of Jonathan and David. From their friendship we learn the following lessons.

I. FRIENDSHIP IS LOVING OTHERS AS YOURSELF (1 SAMUEL 18:1-4)

Evidently Jonathan was greatly moved by such a display of courage by such a young man. Immediately his heart was drawn to David's. Verse 1 tells us that their souls were knit together, and "Jonathan loved him _____."
How did Jonathan show this love? Read verse 4. List five things that Jonathan gave to David.

_____

_____

As Saul's oldest son, Jonathan was the heir apparent to the throne; yet here we read of Jonathan giving gifts to David that would indicate that he recognized David as his father's successor. One would expect Jonathan to be jealous of this young man who was going to take his place on the throne of Israel. Not so with Jonathan. He was a true friend. Why? Because, as we read in verses 1 and 3, he had learned to love David "as his own soul."

II. FRIENDSHIP IS MAKING PEACE WITH THE ENEMIES OF A FRIEND (1 SAMUEL 19:1-7)

When his father wanted to take David's life, what did Jonathan do? Read verses 4 and 5.

_____

_____

According to verses 6 and 7, did this work? _____

III. FRIENDSHIP IS HELPING OTHERS TO FOCUS ON THE LORD (1 SAMUEL 23:16-18)

At a time when David was in a state of discouragement and despair, his friend Jonathan came out in the woods to meet with him secretly. According to verse 16, what did Jonathan do for David?

_____

This means that Jonathan encouraged David to turn his attention to the Lord, focus on Him and recognize that He was his source of hope and strength. Do you do this for your friends?

IV. FRIENDSHIP IS HONORING YOUR COMMITMENTS TO YOUR FRIENDS (2 SAMUEL 9:1-13; 21:1-7)

According to these verses, what commitment that David had made to Jonathan did he continue to honor even after Jonathan's death?

_____

_____

Are you faithful in keeping your promises to your friends? _____

How To Build A Friendship (Part 1)

SIX KEYS TO BECOMING A FRIENDLY PERSON

🔑 _____

Example: _____ (Rom. 5:8)

🔑 _____

Example: _____ (Rom. 15:7)

OUR YOUTH GROUP WOULD BE BETTER OFF WITHOUT *HER!*

IS THIS YOUR YOUTH GROUP?

Example: _____ (Rom. 16)

Example: _____ (Ps. 91:15; Jer. 33:3; Mt. 7:7)

SEVEN RULES OF LISTENING

1. Stop what you are doing.
2. Tell the person you are sincerely interested in what he has to say.
3. Look directly at the person who is talking.
4. Pay attention to what is being said — don't just daydream.
5. Let the person finish and say all he wants to say on the subject.
6. Respond with meaningful comments.
7. Take action! Do whatever you can to help solve any problems the person mentioned during the discussion.

Example: _____ (1 Sam. 23:16)

Example: _____ and _____
(1 Sam. 18:3; 20:16, 42; 23:18; 2 Sam. 21:7)

FRIENDSHIP PROJECT #2

Copy the following chart on another piece of paper. Listed on the chart are the six keys to becoming a friendly person that we studied in the teacher's lesson. Beside each key, circle the number that corresponds to the way in which you are already practicing that guideline. For example, a "10" would mean that you are always doing it, a "7" would mean that you do it most of the time, a "4" would mean you do it some of the time, and so on. Then on the back of this piece of paper, write several paragraphs explaining in detail how you practiced one or more of these guidelines in your life this week. *Your youth director will keep this information confidential, so be honest!* (As with the first friendship project, completing this paper and turning it in to your youth director will earn you 50 bonus points.)

KEY #1—
REACHING OUT TO OTHERS   1 2 3 4 5 6 7 8 9 10

KEY #2—
ACCEPTING OTHERS AS THEY ARE   1 2 3 4 5 6 7 8 9 10

KEY #3—
ENJOYING BEING WITH OTHERS   1 2 3 4 5 6 7 8 9 10

KEY #4—
LISTENING TO OTHERS   1 2 3 4 5 6 7 8 9 10

KEY #5—
ENCOURAGING OTHERS   1 2 3 4 5 6 7 8 9 10

KEY #6—
BEING LOYAL TO OTHERS   1 2 3 4 5 6 7 8 9 10

How To Build A Friendship (Part 2)

Many books have been written during our lifetime telling us how to win new friends. However, none of these books is as important as one which was written thousands of years ago. What book is it? (Be specific.) _____

This lesson will point out some specific proverbs, and in them we will find five qualities that need to be a part of our lives if we want to gain new friends.

I. BE DILIGENT (PROVERBS 11:27)

According to this verse, what are we to be diligent in doing?

_____

This verse teaches us the following.

• There are two types of people:

Those who _____

Those who _____

• You will _____

As was noted last week, friendships don't just happen; they have to be built. And it takes diligent effort on our part to build a good friendship.

II. BE UNDERSTANDING (PROVERBS 13:15)

Most problems are nothing more than misunderstandings. What causes misunderstandings?

THE CAUSE OF MOST MISUNDERSTANDINGS

THE CURE FOR MISUNDERSTANDINGS

To see how important this is, read the following verses and write beside each what it says about the grave consequences of failing to obey this rule.

Proverbs 14:18 _____

Proverbs 14:29 _____

Proverbs 20:22 _____

_____

Proverbs 25:8 _____

_____

III. BE MERCIFUL (PROVERBS 14:21)

What does it mean to be merciful to others? _____

_____

According to Proverbs 10:12 and 17:9, what is one way we can express this quality to others?

_____

What result of showing mercy is mentioned in Proverbs 11:17? _____

_____

According to Proverbs 14:31, what kind of person shows mercy to the poor? _____

_____

According to Proverbs 19:17, what is one of the benefits of being merciful to others?

_____

_____

IV. BE RIGHT WITH GOD (PROVERBS 16:7)

Read Genesis 27:41; 32:6-8 and 33:1-4. How is this truth illustrated in the lives of Jacob and Esau?

_____

_____

Read Exodus 1:11-14; 3:19-22 and 12:29-36. How is this truth illustrated in Israel's exodus from Egypt?

_____

_____

_____

THE BASIS FOR ALL RELATIONSHIPS

```
┌─────────────────────────────────────────────┐
│                                             │
│                                             │
│                                             │
│                                             │
└─────────────────────────────────────────────┘
```

Note the order of the Ten Commandments in Exodus 20.

Relationship to
_____
{
1. No other gods before God
2. Not worship idols or anything other than God
3. Not take the name of the Lord in vain
4. Remember the sabbath day
}

Relationship to
_____
{
5. Honor your father and mother
6. Not murder
7. Not commit adultery
8. Not steal
9. Not lie
10. Not covet
}

Thus, if we are to have right relationships with others, we must begin with a right relationship with the Lord.

V. BE CONSIDERATE (PROVERBS 29:7)

Note the difference in the considerate man and the selfish man.

CONSIDERATE MAN   SELFISH MAN

Psalm 41:1-3   Proverbs 21:13

41:1— _____   _____

_____   _____

_____   _____

41:2— _____   _____

_____

_____

_____

41:3— _____

_____

_____

Ten Ways To Destroy A Friendship

In the past two lessons we have discussed the things we can do to cultivate quality friendships. We have also seen how valuable a good friendship can be. It is only logical that if all of this is true, we should be very careful to identify and avoid anything that would destroy a good friendship. That's what we want to do in this lesson. We are going to study ten things that are potentially fatal to any friendship so that we can all work on keeping these things out of our lives.

SELFISHNESS

First Corinthians 13 gives us the characteristics of love. What characteristic in verse 5 do we see that is the very opposite of selfishness?

_____

What does the Bible say about selfishness in each of the following verses?

• Leviticus 19:18—_____

• 1 Corinthians 10:24—_____

_____

• 2 Timothy 3:1-2—_____

_____

POSSESSIVENESS

What two things cause a person to be possessive?

1. _____

2. _____

JEALOUSY

What is jealousy? _____

_____

Who was jealous of whom in Genesis 37:1-4? _____

_____

Why were they jealous? _____

_____

What sins did they commit because of their jealousy? _____

_____

ANGER

Record below what the Bible says about anger.
- Proverbs 15:1— _____
- Proverbs 22:24— _____
- Colossians 3:8— _____
- 1 Timothy 2:8— _____

HATRED

I DON'T HATE MY FRIENDS; I JUST HATE MY ENEMIES! WHAT'S WRONG WITH THAT? HATING OTHERS WON'T AFFECT MY FRIENDSHIPS WITH THE ONES I LIKE.

How would you answer a statement like that? _____

_____

Look up the following verses and record what they say about the person who has hatred in his heart.

• 1 John 2:9, 11—_____

_____

• 1 John 3:14—_____

• 1 John 3:15—_____

• 1 John 4:20—_____

DISHONESTY

Read Psalm 41:9 and 55:11-14. Who was disloyal to and dishonest with David? _____

_____

Why was David so hurt over his friend's dishonesty? _____

_____

INTOLERANCE

What is intolerance? _____

_____

Read Mark 9:38-40 and answer the following questions.

• What was John's problem? _____

• What reason did he give for not accepting this person? _____

_____

• Did Jesus agree with John's attitude? _____

CRITICISM

Read 1 Thessalonians 5:18. What is the cure for a critical, discontented spirit? _____

_____

List people you are grateful for and write beside their names why you are thankful for them in the following chart.

PEOPLE I'M THANKFUL FOR	WHY I'M THANKFUL
_____	_____
_____	_____
_____	_____

Why not thank God right now for them!

INSENSITIVITY

Insensitivity means not being aware of and showing concern for the needs of others. The best example of this positive quality is in the earthly life of Jesus Christ. Note two examples of His concern and sensitivity toward others.

• Matthew 20:30-34— _____

• Luke 7:11-15— _____

What about you? Are you sensitive to the physical, emotional and spiritual needs of those around you? Do you care? Do you show concern? Do you try to help? This is not only what builds a friendship, but also helps maintain it throughout the trials of many years.

GOSSIP

Someone once said, "Of every ten persons who talk about you, nine will say something bad, and the tenth will say something good in a bad way." Notice what the Bible has to say about the person who gossips.

• Proverbs 11:13— _____

• Proverbs 16:28— _____

• Proverbs 18:8— _____

How many of these ten qualities are in your life? Pray right now and ask God to help you overcome them.

FRIENDSHIP PROJECT #3

Think of at least one time in your life when one of your friendships was shattered. Perhaps you have become friends again with this person; but for at least a brief period of time, your friendship ceased. Write a one-page paper including the following elements.

• A description of why you stopped being friends (What were the circumstances? What did your friend do wrong? What did you do wrong?)
• Which of the ten things that we listed in this student's lesson were responsible for the

breakup? (Probably several were involved.)

• At least five Scripture verses that would be helpful in preventing a similar situation from severing your friendship again

Turn this paper in to your ProTeen director, and you will receive 50 bonus points in your Local Scoring competition.

Healing The Wounds

18

TEACHER'S LESSON

CHRIST'S TEACHING ON _____

CHRIST'S INSTRUCTIONS FOR AN OFFENDED BROTHER
(MT. 18:15-20)

┌─ **WARNING!!** ──────────────────────┐
- Do not be too _____.
- Do not tell _____.
└──────────────────────────────────────┘

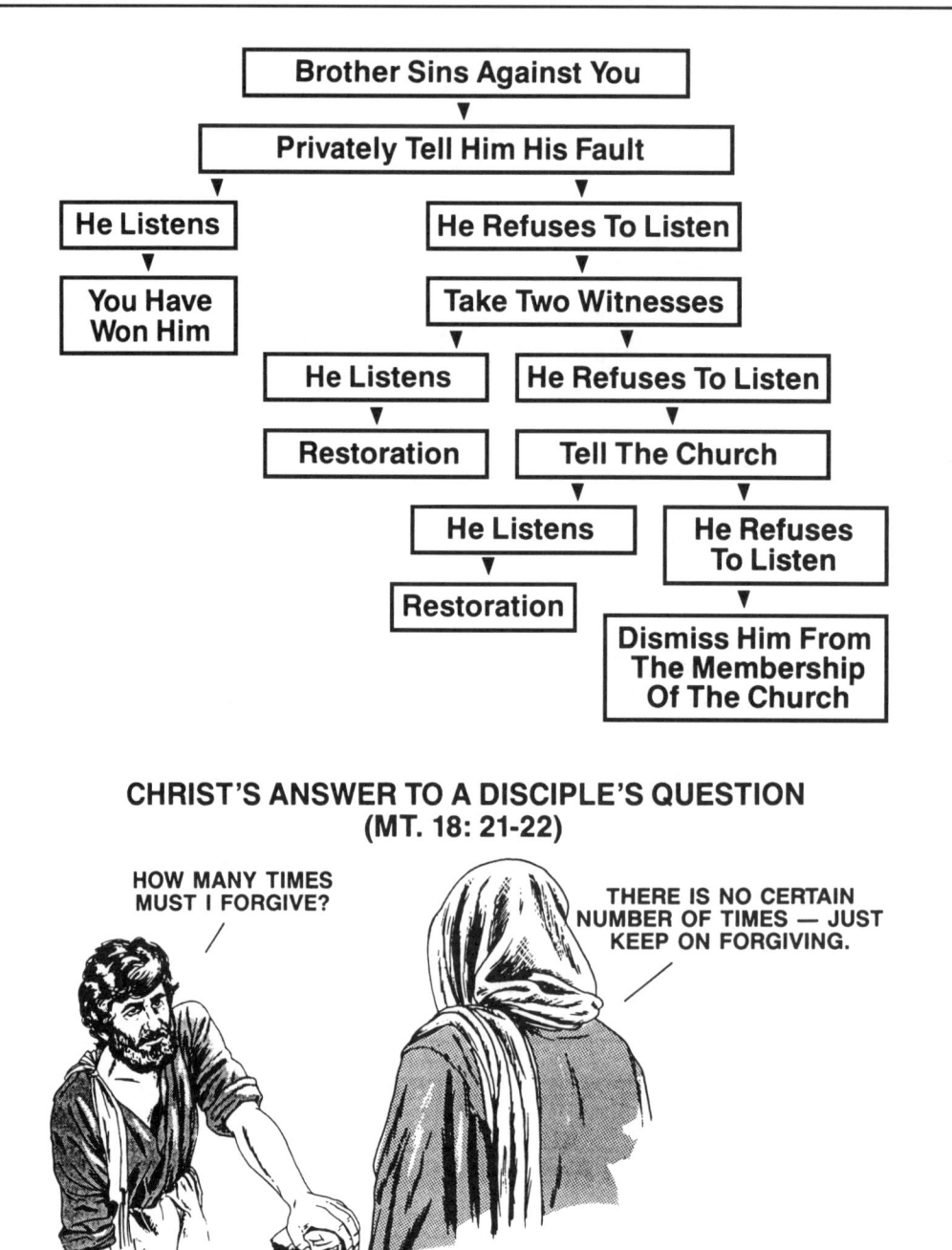

Brother Sins Against You

Privately Tell Him His Fault

He Listens

You Have Won Him

He Refuses To Listen

Take Two Witnesses

He Listens

Restoration

He Refuses To Listen

Tell The Church

He Listens

Restoration

He Refuses To Listen

Dismiss Him From The Membership Of The Church

CHRIST'S ANSWER TO A DISCIPLE'S QUESTION
(MT. 18: 21-22)

HOW MANY TIMES MUST I FORGIVE?

THERE IS NO CERTAIN NUMBER OF TIMES — JUST KEEP ON FORGIVING.

Does a person have to repent before God expects you to forgive that person?

- •   •
- •   •
- •

CHRIST'S PARABLE OF THE UNFORGIVING SERVANT
(MT. 18:23-35)

ACT I (Vs. 23-27)
"The King And His Servant"

_____

ACT II (Vs. 28-30)
"The Servant And One Of His Fellowservants"

_____

ACT III (Vs. 31-35)
"The Servant And His King"

_____

CHARACTERS IN THE PARABLE

King . . . . God
Servant . . . . Us
Fellowservant . . . . Those Who Sin Against Us

LESSONS FROM THE PARABLE

- •NEGATIVELY — If we do not _____ others, it is proof that we ourselves have never been _____ by God.
- •POSITIVELY — When we forgive others, we demonstrate to the world _____.

FRIENDSHIP PROJECT #4

In the teacher's lesson we studied Matthew 18:15-35 to learn what Christ taught about forgiveness. There is a shorter passage in Matthew that has a similar theme. It is similar in that it gives us further instruction concerning what we should do when we have problems in our friendships.

That passage is Matthew 5:23-26. Listed below are definitions of words in the passage that you may have trouble understanding.

- "Bring" = to bring and present offerings or gifts
- "Gift" = offering
- "Hath aught against thee" = to have a grievance against another person
- "Leave" = to leave behind (leave it sitting there and go)
- "Be reconciled" = refers to two people being restored to feelings of good favor toward each other where once there was bitterness and hostility
- "Agree" = make friends with; settle any differences with
- "Adversary" = word used for an opponent in a law case
- "Whiles thou art in the way with him" = while the two of you are on your way to court
- "Deliver" = hand over to; turn custody over to
- "Officer" = the attendant who serves the court and carries out the decisions of the judge
- "Come out thence" = get out of prison
- "The uttermost farthing" = the last penny (This means that if you are thrown into prison, there is no way you will get out until you have paid the last minute portion of your debt—which may imply that you will never get out!)

Once you have read and studied Matthew 5:23-26, write a two-page paper explaining *in your own words* what Christ meant when He said these words and how they apply to your relationships with your friends. Put some time and thought into it, and think of some specific ways to apply these verses to your life. In your paper answer such questions as...

- What does it mean to "be reconciled to a brother"?
- Why must we be right with others before we can be right with God?
- Why is it so important to settle our differences with others "quickly"?

Turn this paper in to your director at the next ProTeen meeting, and you will receive 50 bonus points for Local Scoring.

How To Corrupt Good Morals

19

TEACHER'S LESSON

EVIL _____   CORRUPT GOOD _____

▶ _____   1 Cor. 15:33   ▶ _____

▶ _____   ▶ _____

THEY AFFECT OUR...	SCRIPTURE
	Prov. 13:20
	Prov. 22:5
	Prov. 22:24-25
	Prov. 25:4-5
	Prov. 27:9
	Prov. 27:17
	Prov. 27:19
	Prov. 28:7
	Prov. 28:19

TEN COMPANIONS TO AVOID

WRONG TYPE OF COMPANION	SCRIPTURE
	Prov. 14:15
	Prov. 9:8; 13:1; 15:12
	Prov. 1:7; 13:20
	Prov. 11:13; 16:28; 20:19
	Prov. 22:24-25
	Prov. 24:21
	Prov. 28:7
	Prov. 29:3
	Prov. 3:31
	Prov. 23:20

HOW TO REACH UNSAVED TEENS

Two Extremes

Biblical Balance

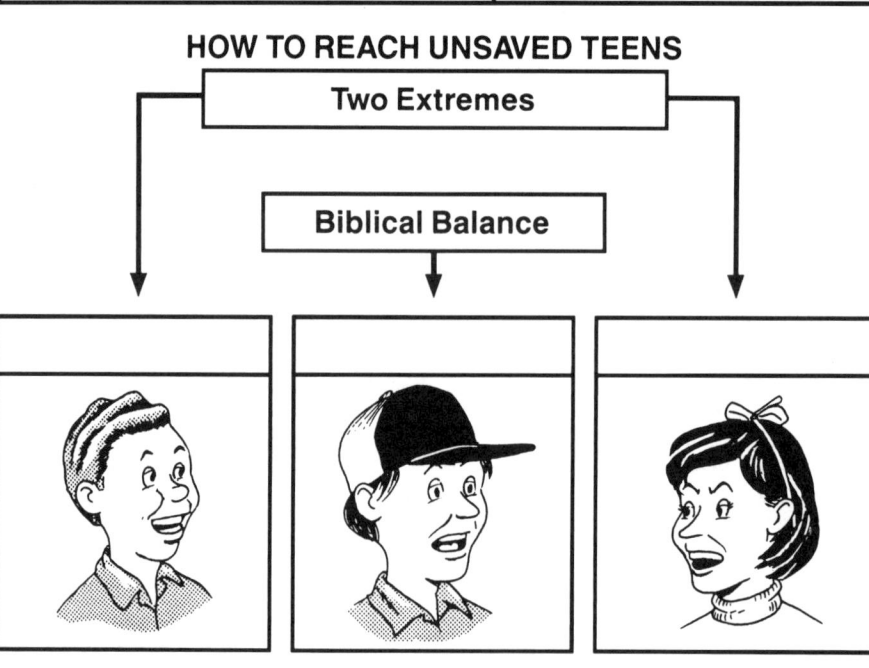

"Sure, I'd love to…"   "Thanks, but…"   "Are you kidding?"

LEVEL ONE *AND* LEVEL TWO

Listed below are sixteen questions from major Bible passages that deal with the subject of how our friendships affect us. So that you will understand what the Bible itself has to say on this subject, read the following verses carefully and answer the question from each verse. Then complete the "search and find" word puzzle containing all the answers to these questions somewhere in the puzzle. Check up on the answers you gave by trying to find them in the puzzle. Keep looking—they are all there!

Note: Some of the answers to these questions may be more than one word. Also, make sure you use the King James Version so your answers will match exactly with the words in the puzzle.

1. What we should not do when enticed by sinners (Proverbs 1:10)—

_____

2. What a froward (crooked, perverse) person is to God (Proverbs 3:32)—

_____

3. Walk with these if you want to be wise (Proverbs 13:20)—

_____

4. The kind of man we should stay away from (Proverbs 14:7)—

_____

5. The kind of man who will lead you down the wrong path (Proverbs 16:29)—

_____

6. This will get you a lot of "friends" fast (Proverbs 19:4)—

_____

7. Where you should be in relationship to the froward (Proverbs 22:5)—

_____

```
D  O  W  E  A  L  T  H  A  Y
T  E  C  X  B  R  O  R  O  O
F  N  C  O  O  J  E  K  D  K
R  E  E  E  M  L  E  D  A  E
E  M  L  S  I  P  P  F  N  D
H  E  P  R  N  T  A  M  E  V
T  S  M  T  A  O  L  N  I  E
O  I  I  B  T  F  C  O  Y  T
R  W  S  L  I  S  L  E  M  H
B  E  A  L  O  E  U  R  E  G
E  A  R  S  N  O  L  S  N  I
A  L  N  T  D  E  F  R  E  L
L  E  I  N  A  D  H  G  I  J
```

8. What we should not do with immoral people (1 Corinthians 5:9)— _____

9. We should not treat a disobedient Christian as a(n) _____ (2 Thessalonians 3:15).

10. We should treat a disobedient Christian as a(n) _____ (2 Thessalonians 3:15).

11. If you practiced this, David would not let you stay in his home (Psalm 101:7)—_____

12. The type of person who is blind to danger (Proverbs 22:3)—_____

13. An example of someone who had convictions without having a contentious spirit (Daniel 1:8)— _____

14. He was called "a friend of sinners" (Luke 7:34)—_____

15. What we should not be with the unsaved (2 Corinthians 6:14)—_____

16. What we should be to the world (Matthew 5:14)—_____

FRIENDSHIP PROJECT #5

In this week's project, we want to focus on how to respond to real-life situations dealing with our friends, how they affect us and how we should respond to them. Read the following brief descriptions and then answer the questions on a separate sheet of paper. Give at least one Scripture reference that supports each of your answers. Turn this paper in to your ProTeen director, and you will receive 50 bonus points for Local Scoring.

1. Sam was totally shocked by the news. He had just heard that one of his best friends in his class had been kicked out of school for experimenting with drugs. What should Sam do now?

2. After Sue heard her pastor preach a message on how important it is to have the right kind of friends, she realized that she needed to make some changes in her life. The friends she had been doing things with were not interested in spiritual things and had encouraged her to do things she knew were wrong. Sue was tired of trying to hide things from her parents and from her youth pastor; she was ready to get things right. What should Sue do now?

3. At the end of the youth rally, the evangelist asked all those who were unsaved to raise their hands. Charles knew he was not supposed to be looking, but he decided he would peek just a little bit. To his surprise, he noticed that Dennis was raising his hand. However, when the invitation was given, Dennis did not go forward. What should Charles do?

4. Bill had just been asked by some of his friends at school to go out with them to eat at a certain restaurant. Bill had heard about what kind of restaurant it was, and he knew that it was no place to be for a Christian who was concerned about his testimony. On the other hand, he did not want to refuse because he felt that his friends might take that as meaning that he thought he was better and more spiritual than they were. What should Bill do?

The Friendship Proverbs

TEACHER'S LESSON

THE FRIENDSHIP PROVERBS

6:1, 3
14:20
16:28
17:9, 17, 18

18:24
19:4, 6, 7
22:11
27:6, 9, 10, 14, 17

| AHEB | ALLUP | MEREA | RAA | REA |

AHEB

Defined	To _____, _____ or be in _____; _____
Translated	• "Love" (___ times) - Prov. 3:12; 13: 24; 22:11 • "Friend" (___ times) - Prov. 14:20; 18:24; 27:6
Proverb	"A friend [aheb] _____, and a brother is born for adversity" (17:17).
Practiced	

ALLUP

Defined	_____
Translated	• "_____" - Prov. 2:17 • "_____" - Prov. 16:28 • "_____" - Prov. 17:9
Proverb	"He that covereth a transgression seeketh love; but he that repeateth a matter separateth _____ [allup]" (17:9).
Practiced	

MEREA

Defined	_____
Translated	"Friends" (Prov. 19:7)
Proverb	"All the brethren of the poor do hate him: how much more do his friends [merea] _____ _____" (19:7).
Practiced	

RAA

Defined	To be _____ or _____; to _____
Translated	"mischief" (4:16); "wicked doer" (17:4); "to do evil" (24:8); "broken" (25:19); etc.
Proverb	A man of many friends _____ _____ [raa], "and there is a friend that sticketh closer than a brother" (18:24).
Practiced	

REA

Defined	_____, _____, _____
Translated	• "Neighbor" (_____ times) • "Friend" (_____ times)
Proverb	"Iron sharpeneth iron; so a man _____ _____ of his friend [*rea*]" (27:17).
Practiced	

A s was mentioned in the teacher's lesson, this lesson is called "The Friendship Proverbs" because it focuses on those proverbs that contain an English or Hebrew word that is used for "friendship." In the teacher's lesson we studied the five Hebrew words that are translated by the English word "friend" in the Book of Proverbs. We also mentioned that there are a total of seventeen different verses in Proverbs that contain the words "friend," "friends" or "friendly." In this student's lesson we will look at most of those seventeen verses.

Each of the clues given below is based on a statement in one of those verses in Proverbs. Remember that each verse has something to say about friendship. Look up the verse for each clue and then record the correct response from the verse in the appropriate squares in the crossword puzzle that follows.

ACROSS

1. What a man does to someone else's offense if he wants to "seek love" (17:9)
4. One who is hated even by his own neighbors (14:20)
6. Where your brother may be in relationship to you (27:10)
9. A man without this is quick to "strike hands" [that is, pledge his possessions as security for someone else's loan] (17:18)
11. Someone you do not want to kiss (27:6)
12. Metals that sharpen each other (27:17)

DOWN

2. Describes the relationship between the poor and his neighbor (19:4)
3. What is sought by someone who overlooks the offenses of others (17:9)
5. When a friend loves [two words] (17:17)
7. Describes the voice of your friend's blessing that turns out to be a curse (27:14)
8. What a boisterous, early blessing from a friend should be considered (27:14)
10. Describes the king's friend's lips (22:11)

FRIENDSHIP PROJECT #6

This last in our series of Friendship Projects gives you a chance to do some creative thinking and writing. Much of what we have studied about in our relationships to our friends has been based on the Book of Proverbs. This project provides you with the opportunity to create some of your own proverbs.

Listed below are some incomplete proverbs that need to be finished. None of them has been copied directly from Scripture, so we are not asking you to look up verses and fill in the blanks. What we are asking you to do is to recall what you have studied about friendships and use what you have learned to complete the following statements. We have done the first one for you to help you get started.

Copy the completed proverbs on a separate sheet of paper and turn them in to your ProTeen director at your next meeting. Doing so will result in 50 bonus points being added to your score in Local Scoring.

1. A good friend is like an arrow; _he is always straight and true._

2. My parents build strong walls around me to _____
_____

3. A good friend smiles and encourages, while a false friend _____
_____

4. Fools always _____, while
wise men _____

5. Like a refreshing summer breeze, a friend _____
_____

6. It is as hard to win back a friend as it is to _____
_____

7. A true friendship is as precious as gold because _____
_____

8. As dynamite to an old building, so _____
totally destroys a friendship.

9. It is better to have one good friend you can count on than to have _____
_____

10. Jesus Christ sticks closer than a brother, and He _____
_____

SHIPS

Scholarship

Relationship to Our School

Why Does God Want Me To Do My Best In School?

GOD WANTS MY BEST IN SCHOOL BECAUSE...

OF THE IMPORTANCE GOD PLACES ON MY MIND

Seven verses Paul wrote about the mind

-
-
-
-
-
-
-

Five doctrines based on knowledge

-
-
-
-

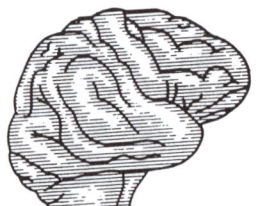

GOD WANTS MY BEST IN SCHOOL BECAUSE...

OF THE IMPORTANCE OF MY CHRISTIAN TESTIMONY

Biblical examples:

- _____ (Acts 7:22)
- _____ and his _____ (Dan. 1:4, 17, 20)
- _____

**IF I ONLY HAD THREE YEARS LEFT
TO SERVE THE LORD, I WOULD SPEND
TWO OF THEM STUDYING AND PREPARING.**

GOD WANTS MY BEST IN SCHOOL BECAUSE...

EVERY SUBJECT TEACHES ME SOMETHING ABOUT GOD

SUBJECT	WHAT IT TEACHES ABOUT GOD
Mathematics	
Science	
History	
Language	
Art	
Music	

Have you ever had someone tell you *what* to do but not tell you *how* to do it? Suppose your father handed you a new oil filter and told you to go out to his car, take out the old oil filter and put in the new one? Would you know what to do? Probably most teenagers would not know what to do first.

The main purpose of the teacher's lesson was to establish one main point—namely, that it is God's will for you at this point in your life that you do your best in school. But it does you very little good to agree with this point if you do not know how to begin practicing it in your life. In other words, the question we must now consider is—"What should I do if I want to do my best in school?"

We will devote the next two student's lessons to answering this question. Some people may not think that sharpening your study skills is spiritual, but anything that will help you obey God's will and fulfill God's plan for your life is definitely spiritual.

I. WHY STUDY

One of the most basic questions to begin with is, "Why should I study?" The most obvious answer to this question is that studying helps us improve our reasoning abilities. Fred Honig in his book, *Taking Tests and Scoring High* (New York: Arco, 1978, page 10), lists five ways that studying can help us improve our intelligence (that is, our reasoning ability). He writes that studying helps us in...

- memory training
- solving mathematical problems and puzzles
- reading books, newspapers and magazines
- adding to your vocabulary by learning a few new words a day
- and above all, just plain thinking...

...and that all five of these things combined help us to increase our intellectual capacity and mental capabilities.

II. WHERE TO STUDY

Once we have determined that we will do our best in studying, we need to decide where we will do most of our studying. Here are a few tips to remember.

■ Select a place where you can study consistently such as a desk in your bedroom. It is important that it be a place where you can set up your materials and leave them there, even when you are called away for a few minutes.

■ Choose to study in a place that is close to the resources you will be using the most. Don't study at the opposite end of the house from your dictionary and encyclopedia.

■ Make sure the temperature of your study area is near a comfortable 68 degrees F.

■ Make sure you have proper lighting that shines directly on your study materials.

■ Choose carefully where you sit in your study room. Do not sit near a window if you are constantly tempted to look outside and daydream.

■ Above all, avoid all distractions. Make sure your study place is a quiet place. Be selective about playing music during your study time. Most often music is more distracting than it is helpful.

III. WHEN TO STUDY

Next you must consider when you will study. Consider the following suggestions.

■ Choose a time when you are most alert and best able to concentrate. This will vary with each individual—for some it is in the morning, for others the afternoon or evening, and for a few the late evening hours are best.

■ Be consistent in the time you choose. Determine that you will spend that time studying, and do not allow anything that is less important to interfere.

■ After a week or so, evaluate the time you have chosen. Is it working? Would another time work out better with your present schedule?

■ Be realistic. Don't try to study for hours and hours. Give yourself hourly breaks. Otherwise, studying will become a chore that you will try to avoid at all costs.

■ Do not eat too much immediately before the time you have planned to study. If you do, the blood that needs to be used by your *brain* will be used by your *belly* for digestion.

■ Give yourself a reward to which you can look forward—a candy bar, a TV program or a phone call to a friend. This will give you something you enjoy to look forward to at the end of a long period of hard study.

■ Make sure that you allow plenty of time for rest. If you study tonight and do not get enough sleep, that will only mean that you will probably use tomorrow's study time to catch up on the sleep you missed the night before.

IV. HOW TO STUDY

Lastly, let's begin to answer the question, "How should I study?" We will note more details about how to study in next week's student's lesson. For this week, we will focus on two important aspects of study—(1) taking notes in class and (2) reading out of class.

A. TAKING NOTES IN CLASS

In this lesson we have been emphasizing the "out of class" aspects of study. However, we must remember that proper study begins *in the classroom.* How can you study for a test if you have not been listening and taking notes in class? (You might answer, "By borrowing someone else's notes." But the fact remains that if you do, that person had to listen in class and take notes. Why not learn to do this for yourself instead of being lazy and depending on someone else?)

Here are some tips that should help you take better notes in class.

■ The most important thing is *learn to listen.* There is a great difference between listening and hearing. Large corporations spend millions of dollars every year just in teaching their employees to do something they should have learned to do while they were in school—listen.

■ Listen for the structure of what the teacher is saying. Listen for words such as "first," "next," "another," "also" and "lastly."

■ Watch your teacher as much as possible. You can learn a lot of things just by watching your teacher's gestures or by paying close attention to what he writes on the chalkboard.

■ Learn to take notes in outline form. Do not try to write everything the teacher says, or soon you will become discouraged when you find that your pen cannot keep pace with his tongue. Remember, the most important thing in note-taking is not the quantity but the quality of your notes.

■ Learn to write in your own system of shorthand. Learn to abbreviate words, but make sure that you will know what your abbreviations stand for a week later.

B. READING OUT OF CLASS

One of the most difficult things for many students is to do their assigned reading, *and get something out of it.* It is no trouble to let their eyes glide across pages of material, but how can they retain what their eyes have seen? Here are some tips that should help you in your reading.

- Preview each chapter before you read it. Look at the major headings. Familiarize yourself with what the chapter seems to be about.
- If possible, mark the book as you read it. However, mark only the most important points to remember. If you make too many marks, then it is hard to distinguish the important from the unimportant.
- The difference between just seeing words and actually reading them is thinking, and the best way to think while you read is to ask questions. Constantly be asking yourself, "Who? Where? When? How? Why? What?" concerning the subject about which you are reading.
- A good vocabulary is essential to good reading.
- Slower reading is not better reading. Slower reading is an indication of reading problems.
- Therefore, eliminate all possible reading problems—e.g., moving your lips as you read, poor eyesight, repeating ideas in your mind as you read them ("mental echo") and, above all, a lack of concentration.
- Increase your reading rate by doing the following.
  - Read by phrases, not words.
  - Reduce the number of times you focus on a line of print by placing a card at the top of the page and gradually moving it downward.
  - Do not allow yourself to go back and re-read what you have already read.
  - Push yourself.
  - Concentrate! Concentrate! Concentrate!

First Things First

TEACHER'S LESSON

IMPORTANT "FIRSTS" IN THE BIBLE

•MT. 5:24 — FIRST _____
_____

•MT. 6:33 — _____ FIRST
_____

•MT. 19:30 — _____
FIRST _____

•LK. 9:59, 61 — _____
FIRST...

•ROM. 1:16 — _____
..._____ FIRST

•1 TH. 4:16 — _____
_____ FIRST

•HEB. 5:12 — _____
_____ FIRST _____

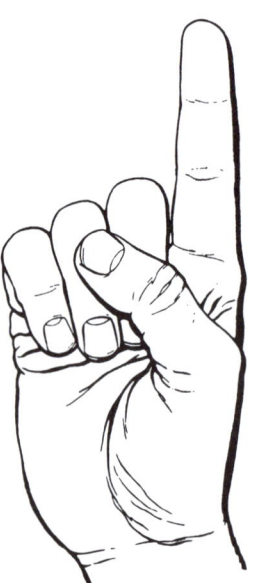

CRITICAL CHOICES IN THE BIBLE

- _____ — Choice of direction
- _____ — Choice of social status
- _____ — Choice of submission

_____ (Heb. 12:1-2)

GUIDELINES FOR ESTABLISHING RIGHT PRIORITIES

GUIDELINE	SCRIPTURE
_____ what is most _____ to you	"Seek ye first the _____ of God and his _____-_____" (Mt. 6:33)
_____ today's activities in the light of _____	"Set your _____ on _____, not on things on the earth" (Col. 3:2)
_____ how much _____ should be allotted for each activity	"_____, because the days are evil" (Eph. 5:16)

The main theme of this week's teacher's lesson was *establishing right priorities*. We learned from Matthew 6:33 ("seek ye first the kingdom of God and his righteousness") that our top priority in life should be our relationship with Jesus Christ. But that does not mean that school work is unimportant. As we learned in Lesson 21, God wants you to do your best in school. That is His will for you at this point in your life. Therefore, part of putting the Lord first and seeking His will is doing your best in school. That is why in this student's lesson we will continue the study we began in Lesson 21 as we try to improve our study skills.

I. WHY GIVE HOMEWORK?

This question must have passed through the mind of every person who has ever been in school. Why do teachers give homework? You may think they give it just to pester you, but there are legitimate reasons why homework should be given.

A. TO ENCOURAGE YOU TO STUDY THINGS OUT FOR YOURSELF

It has been said that the major benefit of going to college is not that you learn a lot of new facts, but that you learn how to study so you can dig out the facts for yourself. The same can be applied to homework. One of the best reasons for giving homework is that it teaches you to dig on your own. It is good to have a teacher tell you what he has studied, but it is much more profitable for you to learn to study for yourself.

B. TO HELP YOU PRACTICE AND APPLY NEW SKILLS

Secondly, homework helps you put into practice what you have learned in the classroom. You may know how to work out every problem in algebra as long as the teacher is standing in front of the classroom and explaining each step. However, you will not always have a teacher around to tell you each step to take, so it is good for you to have work to do at home on your own.

C. TO TEACH YOU TO USE YOUR LEISURE TIME WISELY

Thirdly, homework forces you to keep from wasting time. If you have a certain amount of homework to do each night, you must take the necessary time to accomplish that work. That means forfeiting some trips to the mall or perhaps your favorite TV program. And as you do your work, it doesn't just occupy your time; it actually teaches you new things so that you learn things in math, science, history and literature that you would have never known had you not been forced to do that homework.

II. WHY WRITE PAPERS?

One exercise that many students find to be the most dreaded is that of writing papers. They hate to write because if done correctly, writing requires much time and thought. However, writing will definitely pay off in the long run because there are certain benefits to writing. Notice the following values of learning to write well.

■ Writing calls for exactness. It forces us to put our thoughts into words and to make them correspond precisely to our thoughts and ideas.

■ Writing causes us to think. You cannot write without thinking; and the better the writing, the better the thinking.

■ Writing makes us use our language skills. It makes us ask ourselves, "Should this be singular or plural? Does this call for the nominative or objective case? Is this a participle or a gerund?"

■ Writing necessitates hours of research. You may as well face it—*writing is hard work!* It requires you to spend time researching your subject before you ever write the first word of your paper. However, through all this research you will learn to reason, think and arrive at objective conclusions.

III. HOW TO WRITE PAPERS

Now that we know how writing can help us, let's look at how to write a good research paper. There are six basic steps to follow.

A. SELECT A TOPIC

Do not do this too hastily. Do some reading in the general area in which you plan to write. Become familiar enough with your subject that you can choose a topic that is neither too broad nor too narrow. Then write a thesis statement—that is, write in one sentence what you intend to do in your paper.

B. RESEARCH THE TOPIC

This is the point at which you do your most thorough research of the topic. From the beginning develop a system of exact record-keeping (such as using note cards) so that you know from which source you have derived all your information. If you have trouble finding information, look through bibliographies of books and search out sources that others have already consulted.

C. ORGANIZE YOUR MATERIALS

Go back and reread all of your note cards and allow an outline of your material to begin to develop in your mind. Begin to classify the various aspects of your topic. Bring together all the information you have on each aspect. Then write a complete outline of how you plan to present your topic. Read through your note cards one more time and then evaluate the strengths and weaknesses of your outline in light of the information you have gathered.

D. DO SOME MORE RESEARCH

At this point you will notice some things that you should have mentioned in your outline but omitted. Perhaps there are other topics that are included in your outline, but you realize that you have not done enough research to actually write about them. Therefore, go back to your major sources and do some more research in these areas.

E. WRITE YOUR ROUGH DRAFT

Now you are finally ready to begin writing your paper. Give much time and thought to your introduction and conclusion. Make them interesting and appropriate. Follow each point in your outline and develop it in detail. As you write, make sure you write in your own words and from your own thoughts, giving credit to other writers when necessary. Once you have completed your rough draft, go back and reread it. Be critical of what you have written. Make sure your spelling and punctuation are correct. Strike out any unnecessary phrases or paragraphs.

F. WRITE YOUR FINAL DRAFT

After you have gone over your rough draft very carefully several times, incorporate the changes that need to be made into the writing of your final draft. If possible, type your final draft so that your paper will look as neat as possible.

If you follow each of these six steps, you will have a quality research paper. Above all, you will have the satisfaction of knowing that you have done your best.

SHIPS

Fellowship

Relationship to the Church

An Introduction To The Church

THE FOUNDATION OF THE CHURCH

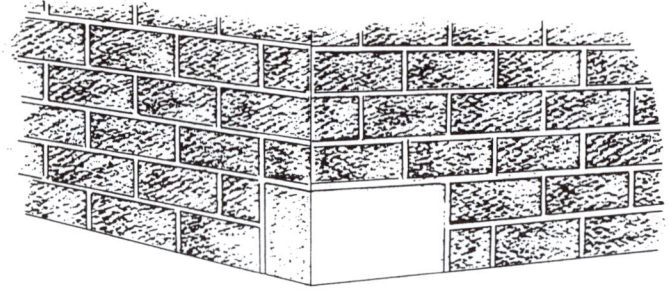

_____

THE DEFINITION OF THE CHURCH

_____   _____

THE FUNCTIONS OF THE CHURCH

_____

_____

_____

THE MISSION OF THE CHURCH

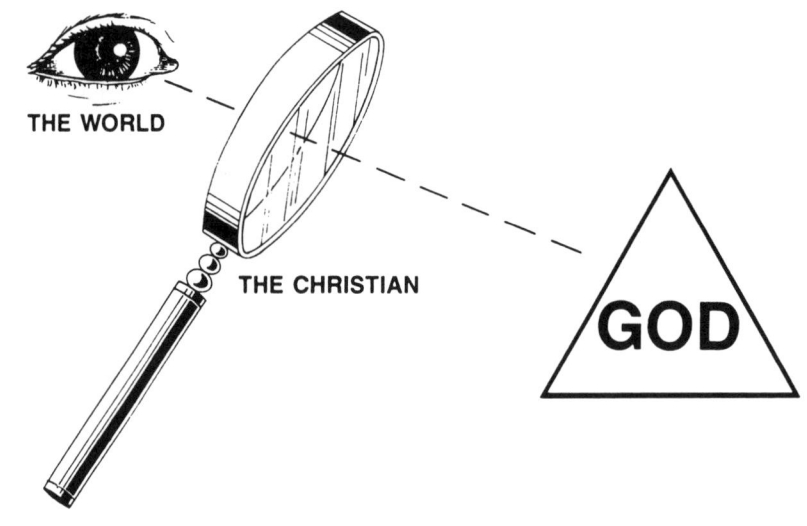

THE WORLD

THE CHRISTIAN

GOD

_____   _____

We mentioned in last week's teacher's lesson that there are two aspects we need to keep in mind when we talk about the church. One is the local church, and the other is the body of Christ. To help us better understand the "body of Christ" aspect of the church, God has provided us with a number of figures or illustrations in His Word. The seven main figures used in the New Testament to refer to the body of Christ are listed below on the right. Match the verses on the left with the correct corresponding figure that each verse describes. (Of course, some of the figures will be used more than once.)

____ 1. John 10:11   A. Christ is the Head; we are the Body

____ 2. John 15:1-8   B. Christ is the Cornerstone; we are the Building

____ 3. 1 Corinthians 15:45   C. Christ is the Bridegroom; we are the Bride

____ 4. 2 Corinthians 5:17   D. Christ is the Shepherd; we are the Sheep

____ 5. Ephesians 2:20   E. Christ is the Vine; we are the Branches

____ 6. Ephesians 5:25-31   F. Christ is the High Priest; we are a Kingdom of Priests

____ 7. Colossians 1:18   G. Christ is the Last Adam; we are a New Creation

____ 8. Hebrews 4:14

____ 9. 1 Peter 2:5, 9

____ 10. Revelation 1:5-6

The Doctrine Of The Church

GOD'S TWO INSTITUTIONS

- Foundation of _____
- If the home _____,
  society _____

- _____
- _____
- _____

THE BELIEVER AND THE CHURCH

■ **The importance of the church**

> **Christ instituted the church as** _____
> _____ .

■ **The finances of the church**

We should give...

- _____ (2 Cor. 8:3, 11, 12)
- _____ (2 Cor. 9:7)
- _____ (2 Cor. 8:2)
- _____ (1 Cor. 16:1-2)
- _____ (1 Cor. 16:2)

HOW SATAN ATTACKS THE CHURCH

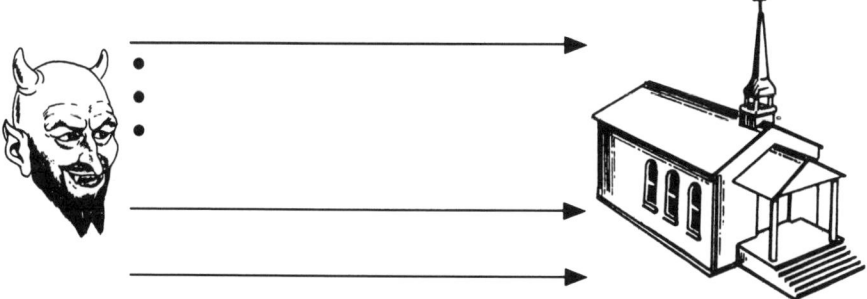

W hat is a church ordinance? An ordinance is *a symbolic rite which sets forth the central truths of the Christian faith.* A rite, in order to be classified as an ordinance, must have been instituted by the specific command of Christ.

To better understand what an ordinance is, it would be well to note the distinctions between the following: a symbol, a rite, an ordinance and a sacrament.

◆ SYMBOL—A sign or visible representation of an invisible truth or idea
◆ RITE—A symbol which is used with regularity by a congregation
◆ ORDINANCE—A symbolic rite (combination of the two above) which sets forth the central truths of the Christian faith
◆ SACRAMENT—A symbolic rite which is believed to convey divine grace and power to the participant (recognized by the Roman Catholic church)

Contrary to the opinions of many, the Bible only prescribes two church ordinances: baptism and the Lord's Supper. Let's examine the significance of both.

I. BAPTISM

A. BAPTISM IS IMPORTANT

How do we see the importance of baptism in the following verses?

Matthew 3:13-17 _____

Matthew 28:19-20 _____

Acts 10:47-48 _____

B. BAPTISM COMES AFTER SALVATION, NOT BEFORE IT

How do the following verses show that baptism follows salvation?

Acts 8:36-38 _____

_____

Acts 16:30-34 _____

_____

Thus, if baptism follows salvation, then we know for sure that baptism cannot save us.

C. BAPTISM IS A PICTURE

According to the following verses, of what is baptism a picture?

Romans 6:3-4 _____

Colossians 2:12 _____

State how each of the following three events is symbolized in baptism.

The death of Christ _____

The burial of Christ _____

The resurrection of Christ _____

STANDING

UNDER

RAISED UP

D. THE MODE OF BAPTISM IS SPECIFIED

What does Acts 8:36-39 indicate about the mode of baptism of the Ethiopian eunuch? Was it sprinkling, pouring or immersion? _____ Even the word "baptism" itself literally means "to immerse."

II. THE LORD'S SUPPER

Read Luke 22:14-20 and 1 Corinthians 11:23-30, and answer the following questions.

What are the two elements of the Lord's Supper?

_____

What do each of the two elements represent? _____

_____

On what night did Christ institute the Lord's Supper? _____

What phrase shows that the Lord's Supper is to be a remembrance of Christ? _____

_____

Until what event are we to continue this ordinance? _____

_____

What historical event do we "show" whenever we partake of the Lord's Supper?

_____

What are the results of partaking of the Lord's Supper without the proper qualifications?

_____

Thus, the two church ordinances (baptism and the Lord's Supper), while not required for salvation, are designed to remind us of our Savior, His sacrifice for us and our present responsibilities to Him. To fail to practice these ordinances as Christ instituted them is to live in disobedience to the Lord.

The Doctrine Of Salvation

WHAT IS SALVATION?

Salvation literally means "to _____, to _____, to _____, to _____ or to _____."

WHY DOES SALVATION EXIST?

• MAN'S _____

_____
_____
_____

• GOD'S _____

HOW IS SALVATION PROVIDED?

■ **God's provision**
- • _____ for the captives (Heb. 2:14-15)
- • _____ for the condemned (1 Pet. 2:24)
- • _____ for the sick (Lk. 4:18, 19, 21)

■ **Man's response**

WHAT MUST I DO TO BE SAVED?

BELIEVE ON THE LORD JESUS CHRIST.

WHAT ARE THE RESULTS OF SALVATION?

■ _____ **instead of bondage**
From sin's _____

_____

_____

■ _____ **instead of weakness**

In the teacher's lesson we studied about the one way that we can become a member of the true church—namely, by salvation through Christ. In this student's lesson we will examine some of the doctrines that accompany the doctrine of salvation.

I. REPENTANCE

The word *repent* means "to change one's mind, thought, purpose and views regarding a matter." It has the idea of turning from going in one direction to begin moving in the opposite direction. Read 1 Thessalonians 1:9, and answer the following.

GOD

REPENTANCE

To whom did the Thessalonians turn?

_____

From what did they turn?_____

Why did they turn? _____

Which came first, turning to or turning from? _____

According to Acts 20:17-21, what was the message Paul testified both to the Jews and also to the Greeks?

_____

_____

According to 2 Peter 3:9, what is God's one desire for all men?

_____

_____

According to 2 Timothy 2:25, how does one gain repentance? _____

_____

According to Luke 13:1-5, what will happen to all those who do not repent? _____

_____

According to Acts 17:30, what is God's command to all men everywhere? _____

According to Romans 2:4, what can lead a man to repentance? _____

_____

II. FAITH

As you learned from Acts 20:21, faith is a counterpart to repentance. Though one must repent, he cannot do so apart from faith. Faith may be defined as "acceptance and complete reliance upon." If one does not exercise faith in Christ as Savior, he will not repent. Look up the following verses, and record the results of exercising faith.

Acts 26:18 _____

Romans 5:1 _____

Galatians 3:26 _____

1 Peter 1:5 _____

III. REGENERATION

Regeneration may be defined as "the impartation of a new and divine life." Regeneration is given a special definition in John 3:3. What is it?

_____

How is regeneration described in John 5:24? _____

_____

How is regeneration described in 2 Corinthians 5:17? _____

_____

_____

According to the following verses, how are we "born again" or regenerated?

John 1:12-13 _____

John 3:6-7 _____

James 1:18 _____

1 Peter 1:23 _____

The Apostasy Of The Church

TEACHER'S LESSON

THE MARKS OF APOSTATES
(1 TIMOTHY 4:1-2)

■ _____
■ _____
■ _____

THE CHARACTERISTICS OF THE APOSTATE AGE
(2 TIMOTHY 3:1-7)

Men shall be...

- _____
- _____ (_____ — lovers)
- _____ (_____ on himself)
- _____ (_____, acts _____)
- _____ (speak _____ of God)
- _____
- _____ (_____)
- _____ (No respect for the _____)
- _____
- _____ (not bound by agreements)
- False _____ (slanderers)
- _____ (_____)
- _____ (brutal and violent)
- _____ of those that are good
- _____ (betray the trust of others)
- _____ (do not think of future results)
- _____ (engrossed in self)
- Lovers of _____ more than _____
- A _____ of godliness without the _____
- They _____ into houses
- _____ facts but never knowing the _____

OUR RESPONSIBILITIES IN AN APOSTATE AGE

We need to know the...

■ _____ (2 Tim. 3:1-9)

■ _____ (2 Tim. 3:10-13)

   • Live _____

   • Be willing to _____

■ _____ (2 Tim. 3:14-17)

SEXUAL FREEDOM   UNSTABLE ECONOMY

DRUGS   DIVORCE

HOMOSEXUALITY   NUCLEAR WAR

I. THE MEANING OF "APOSTASY"

The word "apostasy" is used of a soldier who "deserts his post." When applied to the church, it refers to those who depart from the faith.

The Greek word *apostasia* is found only twice in the New Testament. Notice these two instances.

■ Acts 21:21. Here it is translated "forsake." What did the people "forsake" in this verse?

_____

The background of this verse throws some light on the meaning of the word "apostasy." In this passage the early church leaders are reminding Paul that he was telling the Jewish converts to forsake or "apostatize" from the Jewish tradition and follow the new practices of the church. This turning from the Old Testament rituals to the New Testament church was a form of "apostasy."

■ 2 Thessalonians 2:3. What two words in this verse do you suppose are the translation of the Greek work *apostasia*?

_____

This verse is talking about the turning away from the truth that occurs before the _____

_____ is revealed.

To properly understand the apostasy of the church, we must keep in mind the distinction between the true church of all born-again believers (the body of Christ) and the church as an organization or institution.

• The true church of all true believers will never apostatize or turn from the truth.
• Many local churches, however, will depart from the truth while maintaining the name "church."

For the purposes of this lesson, let us say that the word "apostasy" means *to know the truth and turn from it*. It refers to the time when churches and professing Christians will turn from the fundamental truths of the Word of God and deny them.

II. THE DIVINE COMMANDS FOR THIS AGE

In 2 Timothy 4:1-5, Paul gives some specific instructions for those of us who live in an apostate age. Read these verses, and then answer the following questions.

What five commands are given in verse 2?

(1) _____ the word.

(2) Be _____ (diligent) in season, out of season.

(3) _____ .

(4) _____ .

(5) _____ with all _____ and

_____ .

What will men not endure in the last days? _____

Why will these men "heap to themselves teachers"? _____

_____

Since these men have "itching ears," what kind of teachers do you suppose they will listen to?

_____

To what will these teachers turn their listeners? _____

_____

Paul gives four more commands to true Christians in verse 5 that are especially pertinent to the last days. What are they?

(1) _____ in all things.

(2) Endure _____.

(3) Do the work of an _____.

(4) Make full _____ of thy _____ (that is, be faithful in discharging all your duties as a true minister of Christ).

SHIPS

Lordship

Relationship With The Lord

Who Is The Lord Jesus Christ?

Name:

Defined:

Stated:
- Mt. 1:23 — Emmanuel — _____ }
- Mt. 1:25 — Jesus — _____ }

Applied:
- _____
- _____
   (Ps. 3:8; 37:39; Jonah 2:9)

Name:

Defined:
- _____
- _____

Stated:
Andrew — "We have found the _____, which is, being interpreted _____ "(Jn. 1:41)

Applied:
All _____ and _____ belong to Him.

Name:

Defined:
- _____
- _____

Stated:

Applied:
- It is a _____ of future glory for us
- We can behold _____ now
  - In the _____
  - In the _____
- It causes sin to become _____

Read the following verses and write beside each the name or names of Christ you find in them.

Genesis 49:10 _____

Numbers 24:17 _____

Deuteronomy 18:15 _____

Job 19:25 _____

Isaiah 7:14 _____

Zechariah 6:12 _____

John 8:58 _____

Of the scores of names and titles of Christ found in the New Testament, let's examine one of the shortest yet most profound. What name for Christ appears in John 8:58 (the last two words of the verse)? _____ What name did God use for Himself in Exodus 3:14? _____ This name indicates eternal present tense. This means that there was never a time when God was not. Thus, the name indicates one who (1) never began, (2) will never end, (3) is totally self-sufficient and (4) is complete in Himself. Let's examine these four aspects of Jesus Christ, who is the great I AM.

I. CHRIST NEVER BEGAN

This fact is known as Christ's pre-existence. This term indicates that Christ actually existed before He existed (that is, before He came to this earth as a human being). How is this fact seen in John 1:1-2?

_____

_____

What does Revelation 1:8 say about this? _____

_____

_____

130

II. CHRIST WILL NEVER END

Which of the following passages best teaches that Christ is eternal—Ephesians 3:19; Hebrews 13:8 or 1 John 3:1? _____ Through the eternal Christ we who are saved have an eternal _____ (Ephesians 3:11) and are promised an eternal _____ (Ephesians 3:21).

III. CHRIST IS TOTALLY SELF-SUFFICIENT

Jesus Christ needs nothing that He cannot supply of Himself. While on earth, if He needed a coin for taxes, what would He do? (Matthew 17:24-27)

_____

_____

If He needed wine to drink, what would He do? (John 2:1-11) _____

_____

If He needed to feed 5,000 men and more women and children, what would He do? (John 6:1-14)

_____

_____

Truly such a man never lived who could compare with our Christ! If He were in the midst of a storm, He could stop it immediately. He could stop a funeral and raise the dead. He could simply speak to a tree and dry up its fruit. He could fill a net with so many fish that the net could not hold them. Yes, He could even lay down His own life and take it back (John 10:18). No one else is like our Lord!

IV. CHRIST IS COMPLETE IN HIMSELF

Thus, if we have Christ, we have all we will ever need! Read the following verses in the Gospel of John and state the things Christ said He was. (Therefore, this means that if we know Him, He is all these things to us.)

6:48, 51 _____

8:12 _____

10:7, 9 _____

10:11 _____

11:25 _____

14:6 _____

15:1 _____

Note especially John 15:6. As He is self-sufficient, within ourselves we are deficient and insufficient. Without Him we are like a dead stick lying on the ground. Only as we "_____" in Him (John 15:4) do we bear fruit.

How do we abide in Him? By fellowshipping with Him through meditation in the Word. Through Him we can have all that He is—*and He is everything!* Whether it is peace, mercy, strength, power, victory, grace, consolation or material goods—He has all we need. Then why should we ever turn to the world to meet our needs? Can you think of a good reason?

The Preciousness Of Christ

TEACHER'S LESSON

God's Greatest Concern

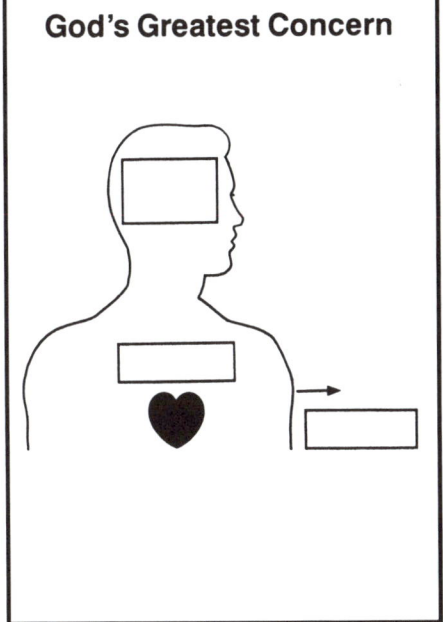

God's Greatest Gifts

- _____
  - ✓ _____ **blessings**
  - ✓ _____ **blessings**
  - ✓ _____ **blessings**
- _____
- _____
- _____

OUR NATURAL RESPONSE

To whom He is not precious	To whom He is precious
• _____	• _____
• _____	
_____	• _____

■ **All the great _____ of the Word center in _____**

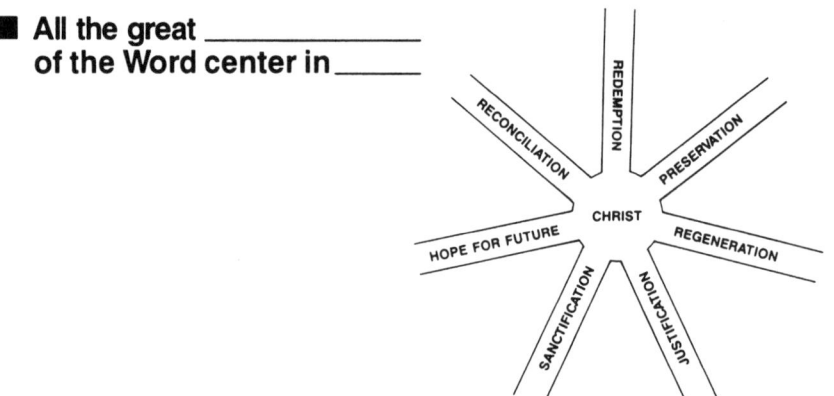

■ **All the _____ and _____ of a Christian reside in _____**

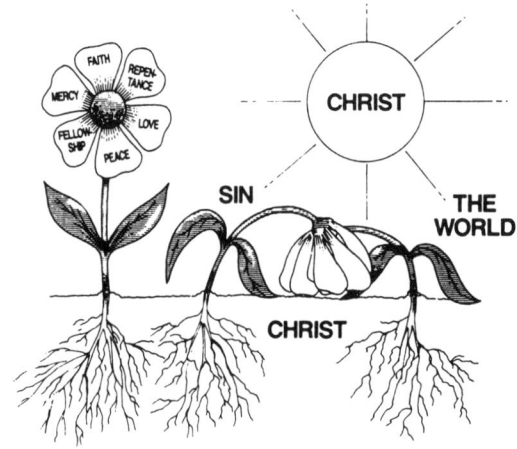

■ **All the fullness of the _____ dwells bodily in _____**

Wꟾe saw in the teacher's lesson that Christ is "precious" to all those that believe (1 Peter 2:7). We learned that the word "precious" signified honor, infinite value and great expense. Since this is true, could Christ have really been precious to us if He were only a man? _____ This points out the great importance of the deity of Christ (the fact that He is fully God). If Christ were not God, He could not rightfully be considered to be "of infinite value."

Therefore in this lesson, we will focus on five major proofs for the deity of Christ. Once we have proven that He is God, then we will also have proven that He deserves to be considered precious by all believers.

PROOF #1—CHRIST IS CALLED GOD

Read the following verses and tell how each states clearly that Christ is God.

Isaiah 9:6 _____

John 1:1 _____

Titus 2:13 _____

Hebrews 1:8 _____

PROOF #2—CHRIST POSSESSES ATTRIBUTES THAT BELONG ONLY TO GOD

Read the following verses, and tell which divine attributes are said to belong to Christ.

Luke 1:35; 4:34 _____

John 2:24-25 _____

Ephesians 3:19 _____

Hebrews 13:8 _____

Revelation 19:11 _____

PROOF #3—CHRIST PERFORMED WORKS THAT ONLY GOD COULD DO

Match the following verses with the corresponding work of God that Christ performed.

135

_____ 1. Matt. 4:23; John 5:36		A. Creating
_____ 2. Matt. 9:2; Luke 7:47-48		B. Performing miracles
_____ 3. Matt. 25:31-32; John 5:22		C. Forgiving sins
_____ 4. John 1:3		D. Giving eternal life
_____ 5. John 10:28		E. Judging men

PROOF #4—CHRIST WAS WORSHIPED AS GOD

Read the following verses and state who refused to be worshiped.

Acts 10:25-26 _____

Acts 14:11-15 _____

Revelation 22:8-9 _____

According to Matthew 4:10, who alone deserves to be worshiped? _____

Since the above facts are true, what do the following verses teach about Christ and the worship that belongs to God alone?

Matthew 14:33 _____

John 5:23 _____

Hebrews 1:6 _____

_____

PROOF #5—CHRIST HIMSELF CLAIMED TO BE EQUAL WITH THE FATHER

How did Christ claim equality with the Father in the following verses?

John 5:18 _____

John 5:23 _____

_____

John 10:30 _____

John 14:9 _____

Christ's Terms Of Discipleship

CHRIST'S HANDLING OF POPULARITY

■ Feeding the 5,000 (Jn. 6:1-14)
- He _____ from the crowd (Jn. 6:15)
- He _____ them (Jn. 6:26)
- He _____ many of them away (Jn. 6:66)

■ Facing would-be followers (Lk. 9:57-62)
- "You may not have _____"
- "Be willing to _____ your family"
- "Leave your _____ behind"

■ Facing the multitudes (Lk. 14:25-33)
"Whosoever does not...cannot be My disciple"

- _____
- _____
- _____

CHRIST'S TERMS OF DISCIPLESHIP

■ Christ first before _____ and _____
_____ (Lk. 14:26)
■ Bear the cross of _____, _____
and _____ (Lk. 14:27)
■ Forsake all _____ (Lk. 14:33)

THE REASONS FOR SUCH ABSOLUTE DEMANDS

■ Christ is _____, and He needs
only the best _____
■ Christ is in a _____, and He needs only the toughest
_____
■ Christ knew _____
in the _____

This lesson concerns itself with Christ's idea of discipleship. The word "disciple" brings two ideas to mind—(1) discipline and (2) following. A disciple is a person who has disciplined himself to follow another. Thus, all good leaders are disciplined to be good followers. This lesson presents Christ's stringent demands on His would-be leaders, emphasizing to them that *the key to being a good disciple of Christ is learning to discipline yourself to follow Him.*

Each of Christ's demands requires certain inner qualities in order for us to meet those demands. Note the following demands and the inner qualities necessary for the accomplishment of each demand.

I. HATRED OF YOUR FAMILY AND YOUR OWN LIFE

THE DEMAND: Christ is obviously not asking us to hate our families. Instead, He is saying that our love for Him should be so great that all other loves appear as hate in comparison.

THE REQUIREMENT: The discipline of our affections. A person must be strong enough to sacrifice that fellowship and closeness of his home situation and such pleasures of life as TV, sports, dates, parties, etc.

II. DENIAL OF SELF

THE DEMAND: There is a difference between self-denial and denial of self. Self-denial means to deny yourself food, clothing, sleep, joys and so on. Christ is not talking about this. On the other hand, denial of self means we must submit our wills to His will. We are commanded to relinquish our right to say "I will do what I want to do" to Him.

THE REQUIREMENT: In order to practice denial of self you must learn to be meek.

III. CROSS-BEARING

THE DEMAND: To take up your cross means that you are to forget popularity and be strong enough to face persecution, mockery, shame and teasing.

I'M GOING WITH MIKE NOW. *HE'S* NOT A CHRISTIAN. HE'S MORE *FUN!*

THE REQUIREMENT: One who takes up his cross must learn to be poor in spirit. We will never bear our cross as long as we are stuck on ourselves.

IV. FOLLOWING CHRIST

THE DEMAND: This is a demand for us to put our eyes on Christ with the intention of pleasing Him rather than seeking to please our own fleshly desires.

THE REQUIREMENT: A heart set on pleasing Christ above self.

V. FORSAKING ALL POSSESSIONS

THE DEMAND: To forget about being rich or having earthly goods in order to be Christ's disciple.

THE REQUIREMENT: A proper set of values. This means we must value godliness more highly than gold.

Are you willing to meet Christ's demands? _____

Are you willing to be His disciple? _____

The First Claim Principle

TEACHER'S LESSON

THE FIRST CLAIM PRINCIPLE

Jesus Christ has _____
_____.

THIS PRINCIPLE IS BASED ON
THREE FACTS ABOUT CHRIST

■ Who He is
  - _____ (Rom. 14:7-11)
  - _____ (Eph. 1:22-23)
  - _____ (Col. 1:15-18)
■ What He has done for us — _____
■ What He is to us — _____
_____

THE APPLICATION OF THE PRINCIPLE
Christ has first claim to our...

C _____ (Ps. 31:15)

L _____ (Mt. 6:33)

A _____ (Col. 3:2)

I _____ (Prov. 3:9)

M _____ (2 Cor. 10:5)